THE LONELY VOICE

FRANK O'CONNOR, pseud.

THE

Lonely Voice

A STUDY OF THE
SHORT STORY

THE WORLD PUBLISHING COMPANY

CLEVELAND AND NEW YORK

Published by The World Publishing Company
2231 West 110th Street, Cleveland 2, Ohio

Published simultaneously in Canada by
Nelson, Foster & Scott Ltd.

Library of Congress Catalog Card Number: 63-8782

FIRST EDITION

Two chapters of this book appeared in the
Kenyon Review before publication.

Contents

633165

"The eternal silence of those infinite spaces terrifies me."

—PASCAL

THE LONELY VOICE

Introduction

"BY THE HOKIES, there was a man in this place one time by the name of Ned Sullivan, and a queer thing happened him late one night and he coming up the Valley Road from Durlas."

That is how, even in my own lifetime, stories began. In its earlier phases storytelling, like poetry and drama, was a public art, though unimportant beside them because of its lack of a rigorous technique. But the short story, like the novel, is a modern art form; that is to say, it represents, better than poetry or drama, our own attitude to life.

No more than the novel does it begin with "By the hokies." The technique which both have acquired was the product of a critical, scientific age, and we recognize the merits of a short story much as we recognize the merits of a novel—in terms of plausibility. By this I do not mean mere verisimilitude—that we can get from a newspaper report—but an ideal action worked out in terms of verisimilitude. As we shall see, there are dozens of ways of expressing verisimilitude—as many perhaps as there are great writers —but no way of explaining its absence, no way of saying, "At this point the character's behavior becomes completely inexplicable." Almost from its beginnings the short story, like the novel, abandoned the devices of a public art in which the storyteller assumed the mass assent of an audience to his wildest improvisations—"and a queer thing happened him late one night." It began, and continues to function, as a private art intended to satisfy the standards of the individual, solitary, critical reader.

Yet, even from its beginnings, the short story has functioned in a quite different way from the novel, and, however difficult it may be to describe the difference, describing it is the critic's principal business.

"We all came out from under Gogol's 'Overcoat'" is a familiar saying of Turgenev, and though it applies to Russian rather than European fiction, it has also a general truth.

Read now, and by itself, "The Overcoat" does not appear so very impressive. All the things Gogol has done in it have been done frequently since his day, and sometimes done better. But if we read it again in its historical context, closing our minds so far as we can to all the short stories it gave rise to, we can see that Turgenev was not exaggerating. We have all come out from under Gogol's "Overcoat."

It is the story of a poor copying clerk, a nonentity mocked by his colleagues. His old overcoat has become so threadbare that even his drunken tailor refuses to patch it further since there is no longer any place in it where a patch would hold. Akakey Akakeivitch, the

copying clerk, is terrified at the prospect of such un-
precedented expenditure. As a result of a few minor
fortunate circumstances, he finds himself able to buy
a new coat, and for a day or two this makes a new man
of him, for after all, in real life he is not much more
than an overcoat.

Then he is robbed of it. He goes to the Chief of
Police, a bribe-taker who gives him no satisfaction,
and to an Important Personage who merely abuses and
threatens him. Insult piled on injury is too much for
him and he goes home and dies. The story ends with a
whimsical description of his ghost's search for justice,
which, once more, to a poor copying clerk has never
meant much more than a warm overcoat.

There the story ends, and when one forgets all that
came after it, like Chekhov's "Death of a Civil
Servant," one realizes that it is like nothing in the
world of literature before it. It uses the old rhetorical
device of the mock-heroic, but uses it to create a new
form that is neither satiric nor heroic, but something
in between—something that perhaps finally transcends
both. So far as I know, it is the first appearance in
fiction of the Little Man, which may define what I
mean by the short story better than any terms I may
later use about it. Everything about Akakey Akakeivitch, from his absurd name to his absurd job, is on
the same level of mediocrity, and yet his absurdity is
somehow transfigured by Gogol.

Only when the jokes were too unbearable, when they
jolted his arm and prevented him from going on with his
work, he would bring out: "Leave me alone! Why do you
insult me?" and there was something strange in the words
and in the voice in which they were uttered. There was a

note in it of something that roused compassion, so that one young man, new to the office, who, following the example of the rest, had allowed himself to mock at him, suddenly stopped as though cut to the heart, and from that day forth, everything was as it were changed and appeared in a different light to him. Some unnatural force seemed to thrust him away from the companions with whom he had become acquainted, accepting them as well-bred, polished people. And long afterwards, at moments of the greatest gaiety, the figure of the humble little clerk with a bald patch on his head rose before him with his heart-rending words "Leave me alone! Why do you insult me?" and in those heart-rending words he heard others: "I am your brother." And the poor young man hid his face in his hands, and many times afterwards in his life he shuddered, seeing how much inhumanity there is in man, how much savage brutality lies hidden under refined, cultured politeness, and my God! even in a man whom the world accepts as a gentleman and a man of honour.

One has only to read that passage carefully to see that without it scores of stories by Turgenev, by Maupassant, by Chekhov, by Sherwood Anderson and James Joyce could never have been written. If one wanted an alternative description of what the short story means, one could hardly find better than that single half-sentence, "and from that day forth, everything was as it were changed and appeared in a different light to him." If one wanted an alternative title for this work, one might choose "I Am Your Brother." What Gogol has done so boldly and brilliantly is to take the mock-heroic character, the absurd little copying clerk, and impose his image over that of the crucified Jesus, so that even while we laugh we are filled with horror at the resemblance.

Now, this is something that the novel cannot do. For

some reason that I can only guess at, the novel is bound to be a process of identification between the reader and the character. One could not make a novel out of a copying clerk with a name like Akakey Akakeivitch who merely needed a new overcoat any more than one could make one out of a child called Tommy Tompkins whose penny had gone down a drain. One character at least in any novel must represent the reader in some aspect of his own conception of himself—as the Wild Boy, the Rebel, the Dreamer, the Misunderstood Idealist—and this process of identification invariably leads to some concept of normality and to some relationship—hostile or friendly—with society as a whole. People are abnormal insofar as they frustrate the efforts of such a character to exist in what he regards as a normal universe, normal insofar as they support him. There is not only the Hero, there is also the Semi-Hero and the Demi-Semi-Hero. I should almost go so far as to say that without the concept of a normal society the novel is impossible. I know there are examples of the novel that seem to contradict this, but in general I should say that it is perfectly true. The President of the Immortals is called in only when society has made a thorough mess of the job.

But in "The Overcoat" this is not true, nor is it true of most of the stories I shall have to consider. There is no character here with whom the reader can identify himself, unless it is that nameless horrified figure who represents the author. There is no form of society to which any character in it could possibly attach himself and regard as normal. In discussions of the modern novel we have come to talk of it as the

novel without a hero. In fact, the short story has never
had a hero.

What it has instead is a submerged population
group—a bad phrase which I have had to use for
want of a better. That submerged population changes
its character from writer to writer, from generation to
generation. It may be Gogol's officials, Turgenev's
serfs, Maupassant's prostitutes, Chekhov's doctors and
teachers, Sherwood Anderson's provincials, always
dreaming of escape.

> "Even though I die, I will in some way keep defeat from
> you," she cried, and so deep was her determination that her
> whole body shook. Her eyes glowed and she clenched her
> fists. "If I am dead and see him becoming a meaningless
> drab figure like myself, I will come back," she declared.
> "I ask God now to give me that privilege. I will take any
> blow that may fall if but this my boy be allowed to express
> something for us both." Pausing uncertainly, the woman
> stared about the boy's room. "And do not let him become
> smart and successful either," she added vaguely.

This is Sherwood Anderson, and Anderson writing
badly for him, but it could be almost any short-story
writer. What has the heroine tried to escape from?
What does she want her son to escape from? "Defeat"
—what does that mean? Here it does not mean mere
material squalor, though this is often characteristic of
the submerged population groups. Ultimately it seems
to mean defeat inflicted by a society that has no sign
posts, a society that offers no goals and no answers.
The submerged population is not submerged entirely
by material considerations; it can also be submerged
by the absence of spiritual ones, as in the priests and
spoiled priests of J. F. Powers' American stories.

Always in the short story there is this sense of out-lawed figures wandering about the fringes of society, superimposed sometimes on symbolic figures whom they caricature and echo—Christ, Socrates, Moses. It is not for nothing that there are famous short stories called "Lady Macbeth of the Mtsensk District" and "A Lear of the Steppes" and—in reverse—one called "An Akoulina of the Irish Midlands." As a result there is in the short story at its most characteristic something we do not often find in the novel—an intense awareness of human loneliness. Indeed, it might be truer to say that while we often read a familiar novel again for companionship, we approach the short story in a very different mood. It is more akin to the mood of Pascal's saying: *Le silence éternel de ces espaces infinis m'effraie.*

I have admitted that I do not profess to understand the idea fully: it is too vast for a writer with no critical or historical training to explore by his own inner light, but there are too many indications of its general truth for me to ignore it altogether. When I first dealt with it I had merely noticed the peculiar geographical distribution of the novel and the short story. For some reason Czarist Russia and modern America seemed to be able to produce both great novels and great short stories, while England, which might be called without exaggeration the homeland of the novel, showed up badly when it came to the short story. On the other hand my own country, which had failed to produce a single novelist, had produced four or five storytellers who seemed to me to be first-rate.

I traced these differences very tentatively, but—on the whole, as I now think, correctly—to a difference in the national attitude toward society. In America as in Czarist Russia one might describe the intellectual's attitude to society as "It may work," in England as "It must work," and in Ireland as "It can't work." A young American of our own time or a young Russian of Turgenev's might look forward with a certain amount of cynicism to a measure of success and influence; nothing but bad luck could prevent a young Englishman's achieving it, even today; while a young Irishman can still expect nothing but incomprehension, ridicule, and injustice. Which is exactly what the author of *Dubliners* got.

The reader will have noticed that I left out France, of which I know little, and Germany, which does not seem to have distinguished itself in fiction. But since those days I have seen fresh evidence accumulating that there was some truth in the distinctions I made. I have seen the Irish crowded out by Indian storytellers, and there are plenty of indications that they in their turn, having become respectable, are being outwritten by West Indians like Samuel Selvon.

Clearly, the novel and the short story, though they derive from the same sources, derive in a quite different way, and are distinct literary forms; and the difference is not so much formal (though, as we shall see, there are plenty of formal differences) as ideological. I am not, of course, suggesting that for the future the short story can be written only by Eskimos and American Indians: without going so far afield, we have plenty of submerged population groups. I am suggesting strongly that we can see in it an attitude of mind that is attracted by submerged population groups, whatever these may be at any given time—tramps, artists, lonely idealists, dreamers, and spoiled priests. The novel can still adhere to the classical concept of civilized society, of man as an animal who lives in a community, as in Jane Austen and Trollope it obviously does; but the short story remains by its very nature remote from the community—romantic, individualistic, and intransigent.

But formally as well the short story differs from the novel. At its crudest you can express the difference merely by saying that the short story is short. It is not necessarily true, but as a generalization it will do well enough. If the novelist takes a character of any interest and sets him up in opposition to society, and then, as a result of the conflict between them, allows his character either to master society or to be mastered by it, he has done all that can reasonably be expected of him. In this the element of Time is his greatest asset; the chronological development of character or incident is essential form as we see it in life, and the novelist flouts it at his own peril.

For the short-story writer there is no such thing as essential form. Because his frame of reference can never be the totality of a human life, he must be forever selecting the point at which he can approach it, and each selection he makes contains the possibility of a new form as well as the possibility of a complete fiasco. I have illustrated this element of choice by reference to a poem of Browning's. Almost any one of his great dramatic lyrics is a novel in itself but caught in a single moment of peculiar significance— Lippo Lippi arrested as he slinks back to his monastery in the early morning, Andrea Del Sarto as he resigns himself to the part of a complaisant lover, the Bishop dying in St. Praxed's. But since a whole lifetime must be crowded into a few minutes, those minutes must be carefully chosen indeed and lit by an unearthly glow, one that enables us to distinguish present, past, and future as though they were all contemporaneous. Instead of a novel of five hundred pages about the Duke of Ferrara, his first and second wives and the peculiar death of the first, we get fifty-odd lines in which the Duke, negotiating a second marriage, describes his first, and the very opening lines make our blood run cold:

> That's my last Duchess painted on the wall,
> Looking as if she were alive.

This is not the essential form that life gives us; it is organic form, something that springs from a single detail and embraces past, present, and future. In some book on Parnell there is a horrible story about the death of Parnell's child by Kitty O'Shea, his mistress, when he wandered frantically about the house like a ghost, while Willie O'Shea, the complaisant husband, gracefully received the condolences of visitors. When you read that, it should be unnecessary to read the whole sordid story of Parnell's romance and its tragic ending. The tragedy is there, if only one had a Browning or a Turgenev to write it. In the standard composition that the individual life presents, the storyteller must always be looking for new compositions that enable him to suggest the totality of the old one.

Accordingly, the storyteller differs from the novelist in this: he must be much more of a writer, much more of an artist—perhaps I should add, considering the examples I have chosen, more of a dramatist. For that, too, I suspect, has something to do with it. One savage story of J. D. Salinger's, "Pretty Mouth and Green My Eyes," echoes that scene in Parnell's life in a startling way. A deceived husband, whose wife is out late, rings up his best friend, without suspecting that the wife is in the best friend's bed. The best friend consoles him in a rough-and-ready way, and finally the deceived husband, a decent man who is ashamed of his own outburst, rings again to say that the wife has come home, though she is still in bed with her lover.

Now, a man can be a very great novelist as I believe Trollope was, and yet be a very inferior writer. I am not sure but that I prefer the novelist to be an inferior dramatist; I am not sure that a novel could stand the impact of a scene such as that I have quoted from Parnell's life, or J. D. Salinger's story. But I cannot think of a great storyteller who was also an inferior writer, unless perhaps Sherwood Anderson, nor of any at all who did not have the sense of theater. This is anything but the recommendation that it may seem, because it is only too easy for a short-story writer to become a little too much of an artist. Hemingway, for instance, has so studied the artful approach to the significant moment that we sometimes end up with too much significance and too little information. I have tried to illustrate this from "Hills Like White Elephants." If one thinks of this as a novel one sees it as the love story of a man and a woman which begins to break down when the man, afraid of responsibility, persuades the woman to agree to an abortion which she believes to be wrong. The development is easy enough to work out in terms of the novel. He is an American, she perhaps an Englishwoman. Possibly he has responsibilities already—a wife and children elsewhere, for instance. She may have had some sort of moral upbringing, and perhaps in contemplating the birth of the child she is influenced by the expectation that her family and friends will stand by her in her ordeal.

Hemingway, like Browning in "My Last Duchess," chooses one brief episode from this long and involved story, and shows us the lovers at a wayside station on the Continent, between one train and the next, as it were, symbolically divorced from their normal surroundings and friends. In this setting they make a decision which has already begun to affect their past life and will certainly affect their future. We know that the man is American, but that is all we are told about him. We can guess the woman is not American, and that is all we are told about her. The light is focused fiercely on that one single decision about the abortion. It is the abortion, the whole abortion, and nothing but the abortion. We, too, are compelled to make ourselves judges of the decision, but on an abstract level. Clearly, if we knew that the man had responsibilities elsewhere, we should be a little more sympathetic to him. If, on the other hand, we knew that he had no other responsibilities, we should be even less sympathetic to him than we are. On the other hand, we should understand the woman better if we knew whether she didn't want the abortion because she thought it wrong or because she thought it might loosen her control of the man. The light is admirably focused but it is too blinding; we cannot see into the shadows as we do in "My Last Duchess."

> She had
> A heart—how shall I say?—too soon made glad,
> Too easily impressed; she liked whate'er
> She looked on, and her looks went everywhere.

And so I should say Hemingway's story is brilliant but thin. Our moral judgment has been stimulated, but our moral imagination has not been stirred, as it is stirred in "The Lady With the Toy Dog" in which we are given all the information at the disposal of the author which would enable us to make up our minds about the behavior of his pair of lovers. The comparative artlessness of the novel does permit the author to give unrestricted range to his feelings occasionally—to *sing;* and even minor novelists often sing loud and clear for several chapters at a time, but in the short story, for all its lyrical resources, the singing note is frequently absent.

That is the significance of the difference between the *conte* and the *nouvelle* which one sees even in Turgenev, the first of the great storytellers I have studied. Essentially the difference depends upon precisely how much information the writer feels he must give the reader to enable the moral imagination to function. Hemingway does not give the reader enough. When that wise mother Mme. Maupassant complained that her son, Guy, started his stories too soon and without sufficient preparation, she was making the same sort of complaint.

But the *conte* as Maupassant and even the early

Chekhov sometimes wrote it is too rudimentary a form for a writer to go very far wrong in; it is rarely more than an anecdote, a *nouvelle* stripped of most of its detail. On the other hand the form of the *conte* illustrated in "My Last Duchess" and "Hills Like White Elephants" is exceedingly complicated, and dozens of storytellers have gone astray in its mazes. There are three necessary elements in a story—exposition, development, and drama. Exposition we may illustrate as "John Fortescue was a solicitor in the little town of X"; development as "One day Mrs. Fortescue told him she was about to leave him for another man"; and drama as "You will do nothing of the kind," he said.

In the dramatized *conte* the storyteller has to combine exposition and development, and sometimes the drama shows a pronounced tendency to collapse under the mere weight of the intruded exposition—"As a solicitor I can tell you you will do nothing of the kind," John Fortescue said. The extraordinary brilliance of "Hills Like White Elephants" comes from the skill with which Hemingway has excluded unnecessary exposition; its weakness, as I have suggested, from the fact that much of the exposition is not unnecessary at all. Turgenev probably invented the dramatized *conte*, but if he did, he soon realized its dangers because in his later stories, even brief ones like "Old Portraits," he fell back on the *nouvelle*.

The ideal, of course, is to give the reader precisely enough information, and in this again the short story differs from the novel, because no convention of length ever seems to affect the novelist's power to tell us all we need to know. No such convention of length seems to apply to the short story at all. Maupassant often began too soon because he had to finish within two thousand words, and O'Flaherty sometimes leaves us with the impression that his stories have either gone on too long or not long enough. Neither Babel's stories nor Chekhov's leave us with that impression. Babel can sometimes finish a story in less than a thousand words, Chekhov can draw one out to eighty times the length.

One can put this crudely by saying that the form of the novel is given by the length; in the short story the length is given by the form. There is simply no criterion of the length of a short story other than that provided by the material itself, and either padding to bring it up to a conventional length or cutting to bring it down to a conventional length is liable to injure it. I am afraid that the modern short story is being seriously affected by editorial ideas of what its length should be. (Like most storytellers, I have been told that "nobody reads anything longer than three thousand words.") All I can say from reading Turgenev, Chekhov, Katherine Anne Porter, and others is that the very term "short story" is a misnomer. A great story is not necessarily short at all, and the conception of the short story as a miniature art is inherently false. Basically, the difference between the short story and the novel is not one of length. It is a difference between pure and applied storytelling, and in case someone has still failed to get the point, I am not trying to decry applied storytelling. Pure storytelling is more artistic, that is all, and in storytelling I am not sure how much art is preferable to nature.

Nor am I certain how one can apply this distinction

if one can apply it at all. In trying to distinguish between Turgenev's novels and *nouvelles*, Dmitry Mirsky has suggested that the *nouvelles* omit conversations about general ideas which were popular in the nineteenth-century Russian novel. I have tried to assimilate this to my own vague feelings on the subject by suggesting that this is merely another way of saying that the characters in the *nouvelles* were not intended to have general significance. In a marvelous story like "Punin and Baburin," the two principal characters seem to have no general significance at all as they would have been bound to have had they been characters in a novel. In fact when they do appear in a novel like "On the Eve" they have considerable general significance, and the reader is bound to take sides between them. The illegitimate defender of human liberty and the gas-bag poet are not people we take sides with. We sympathize and understand, all right, but they both remain members of a submerged population, unable to speak for themselves.

Even in Chekhov's "Duel," that fantastic short story which is longer than several of Turgenev's novels, the characters are too specific, too eccentric for any real generalization, though generalized conversations are strewn all over the place. We look at Laevsky and Nadyezhda Fyodorovna as we look at Punin and Baburin, from outside, with sympathy and understanding but still feeling, however wrongly, that their problems are their own, not ours. What Turgenev and Chekhov give us is not so much the brevity of the short story compared with the expansiveness of the novel as the purity of an art form that is motivated by its own necessities rather than by our convenience.

As I have said, this is not all gain. Like the Elizabethan drama the novel is a great popular art, and full
of the impurities of a popular art, but, like the Elizabethan drama, it has a physical body which a purer
art like the short story is constantly in danger of
losing. I once tried to describe my own struggle with
the form by saying that "Generations of skilful stylists
from Chekhov to Katherine Mansfield and James
Joyce had so fashioned the short story that it no longer
rang with the tone of a man's voice speaking." Even in
the nineteenth century there were writers who seem to
have had the same uncomfortable feeling. One is
Leskov, the only great Russian writer whose work has
not been adequately translated.

Even from the miserable number of his stories that
have been translated it is clear that he wanted literature to have a physical body. He has tried to revive
the art of the folk storyteller so that we can hear the
tone of a man's voice speaking. The folk storyteller,
because his audience (like a child listening to a bedtime story) can only apprehend a few sentences at
a time, unlike a reader who can hold a score of details
before his mind simultaneously, has only one method
of holding its attention, and that is by piling incident
on incident, surprise on surprise. One old folk storyteller, who got someone to read him a couple of my
stories, said sadly, "There aren't enough marvels in
them." In Leskov's "Enchanted Wanderer" he would
have found enough marvels to satisfy even him.

Leskov had also the popular taste for excess. He
liked people to be full-blooded. When they were
drunk he liked them very drunk, and when they fell

in love he did not care for them to be too prudent. "Lady Macbeth of the Mtsensk District" is no understatement as a title. The heroine, consumed by passion, first murders her father-in-law, then her husband, then her co-heir, and finally in destroying herself murders her lover's mistress as well. I think my old friend the folk storyteller would have smacked his lips over that, but I cannot bear to imagine his disappointment over "The Lady With the Toy Dog." "And no one got killed at all?" I can almost hear him cry. He could not have told it to an audience in his little cottage without adding two farcical incidents, two murders, and at least one ghost.

But if this were all, Leskov would be merely a Russian Kipling, and so far as my understanding of his work goes, beyond the superficial resemblances— the episodic treatment and the taste for excess—he had very little in common with Kipling. Kipling, I should say, took the superficial things that belong to oral storytelling without that peculiar sense of the past that illuminates its wildest extravagances. In one very amusing story Kipling describes the native descendants of an Irish rebel in the British forces in India singing "The Wearing of the Green" before a Crucifix and a cap badge at the time of the Angelus, but in his usual way he vulgarizes it, throwing the Crucifix, the Angelus, the cap badge, and the Irish rebel song in with the mutilation of cattle as the essential Irish things— a mistake that Leskov would not have made. Superficially, there is little to distinguish Leskov's "Lady Macbeth" from "Love-O'-Women," but you could put the former into an Icelandic family saga without anyone's noticing anything peculiar about it. Try to think of someone putting the latter in without someone's noticing that "I'm dyin', Aigypt, dyin'" is not the language of saga! It is irremediably the language of the gin palace.

No, Leskov is important because he is really defining a difference of outlook not between an English Conservative and an English Labour man but between two types of human being. Kipling loves the physical only if the physical happens to be his side and to be well equipped with repeating rifles. Leskov loves it for his own sweet sake. Both to Turgenev and to Chekhov flogging was a horror—to Turgenev because he felt that history had cast him for the part of the flogger, to Chekhov, the slave's grandson, because he felt that every blow of the whip was directed at his own back. Leskov, without prejudice—we might as well face it found the whole vile business vastly entertaining. To him flogging was an endurance test like any other, and the essence of masculinity was the capacity to endure. He would probably have defended torture on the same grounds.

> They gave me a terrible flogging, so that I could not even stand on my feet afterwards, and they carried me to my father on a piece of straw matting, but I didn't mind that very much; what I did mind was the last part of my sentence, which condemned me to go down on my knees and knock stones into a garden path. . . . I felt so bad about it that after vainly casting about in my mind how to find a way out of my trouble I decided to do away with myself.

That is an extraordinary attitude which you can find in at least one other story of Leskov's, and quite characteristic of him. For instance when the hero of "The Enchanted Wanderer" has gambled away his boss's money he realizes that the only punishment that fits his case is a flogging, so he goes to his boss with bowed head.

> "What are you up to now?" he asked.
> "Give me a good beating at any rate, sir," I said.

Now, this is not mock-heroics; it is not the maunderings of a sexual pervert; it is identical with the extraordinary scene in Gauguin's *Journal* when his mistress, who has been unfaithful to him, asks to be beaten, not so much because she feels any particular guilt about her own behavior as that she knows instinctively that Gauguin will feel better afterward. It is part of the primitive childish psychology of Lawrence's "Tickets, Please!" and between grown-up, civilized people there is literally nothing to be said about it. It is a fact of childish and primitive psychology, but it means that Leskov is often right about that when liberals and humanitarians like Turgenev and Chekhov are wrong.

It must be twenty years since I read a story of Leskov's called "The Stinger" that reminded me at once of Chekhov's "At the Villa." Chekhov's is a tragic story of a civilized engineer who, with his wife and family, is trying to do everything for the unenlightened peasants about him but incurs their scorn, and is driven out of his home by their malice. Leskov's, as best I can remember it, is about a civilized English factory manager in Russia who replaces the barbaric floggings with mild and meaningless punishments. The peasants, who had hoped that the Englishman would treat them like a father and beat them when they did wrong, are absolutely horrified when they are bidden to stand in a corner, and finally, in despair, burn the Englishman's home about him. The same story, but this time told from inside.

Once again, we could argue till the cows came home and get no nearer a solution. The principal difference is that Leskov, by his very extravagance, convinces us that he knows the peasants, while Chekhov, the saintly doctor, trying to help them from without, simply has no clue to the workings of their minds. Russian and all as he is, he is simply an alien in the world of Leskov and Gauguin.

I do not like that world, but about certain things Leskov is the truer artist.

The battle has gone against the traditionalists, and for the reason which I stated in the opening paragraphs of this chapter. The form itself is modern. It is possible to give a primitive art like the theater a new slant in the direction of a more public statement, but experiment in storytelling is nearly always in the other direction. Leskov, as great a writer as Chekhov if one accepts the views of Russian critics, is practically unknown outside Russia. Kipling, a remarkable storyteller with some of Leskov's virtues, has had little influence outside the English-speaking countries, and even in them it would be hard to deduce from the work of any serious storyteller that such a writer as Kipling had ever existed. Even in his own country he has had no influence on Lawrence, Coppard, or Pritchett.

In Ireland, one could certainly deduce his influence on Edith Somerville and Martin Ross, the authors of *The Irish R.M.,* but the history of their work in their own country is almost an object lesson in the way storytelling develops.

The Irish R.M.—to adopt a general title for the books of stories that began with "Some Experiences of an Irish R.M."—is one of the most lovable books I know. Edith Somerville was an art student in Paris and came under the influence of the French Naturalists, as we can see from a novel like *The Real Charlotte*. George Moore, another member of the Irish landowning class, was also an art student, and also came under the influence of Naturalism, and his novel *Muslin* stands comparison with *The Real Charlotte*. But there the similarity ends. When Somerville and Ross wrote stories, they forgot all they had ever learned from the French Naturalists and apparently wrote just to enjoy themselves. George Moore did not forget, and the influence of Flaubert, Zola, and the Goncourts— even of Turgenev—can be seen even in the slightest of the stories in *The Untilled Field*.

The contrast between these two books is extraordinary. I have reread *The Irish R.M.* off and on for forty years for the mere pleasure of it. The stories in it are yarns, pure and simple. They have a few of the virtues of Leskov's stories; they are of the open air, of horses and animals, and people who have much in common with both. The humor is of the slapstick variety I remember from boys' books of my childhood. The supreme moment of fun comes when the hero breaks his eyeglasses or puts his foot through the barometer. The number of mishaps that occur at the local agricultural show pass all reckoning. The water jump dries up and the distracted stewards fill it with lime.

If, as I suppose, the object was to delude the horses into the belief that it was a water jump, it was a total failure; they immediately decided it was a practical joke, dangerous and in indifferent taste. If, on the other side, a variety entertainment for the public was aimed at, nothing could have been more successful. Every known class of refusal was successfully exhibited. One horse endeavoured to climb the rails into the Grand Stand; another, having stopped dead at the critical point, swung round and returned in consternation to the starting point, with his rider hanging like a locket round his neck. Another, dowered with a sense of humour unusual among horses, stepped delicately over the furze-bushes, and amidst rounds of applause, walked through the lime with stoic calm. . . .

It is only when one asks oneself what the stories are about that one begins to have doubts of one's own judgment. There, indeed, is a man's voice speaking—or a woman's and it calls for an audience, but take the audience away and what are we left with? Nothing, certainly, that responds to analysis. Years ago, I was disturbed by the reading of one story called "Harrington's" and sat down to analyze it. It turned out to be a funny story crossed with a ghost story, and the result resembled a bad accident at a level crossing. The Chimney Sweep comes to the home of the Resident Magistrate, and, knowing the nature of sweeps, the R.M. and his family leave home for the day, having first refused the loan of their long ladder to a humorous neighbor. They call on two spinsters who run a chicken farm and eventually find them at an auction in Harrington's, the house of a mine manager who has committed suicide. One of the spinsters is playing the piano while beside her stands a man in a yachting cap. While the R.M. is purchasing another long ladder (to lend to the neighbor as requested) his little boy disappears, and the spinster confesses to having seen him cross the fields with a man in a yachting cap.

At this point it is obvious to the meanest intelligence that the man in the yachting cap is the deceased mine manager and that he intends some harm to the R.M.'s little boy. The child is rescued with nothing worse than a broken collarbone, and at this point the R.M. discovers that the ladder he has just bought for thirty shillings is his own.

In a story like this, of course, there is scarcely a hint of a work of art. It has no intellectual framework and is nothing when studied alone by the cold light of day. It needs candles and firelight and above all a receptive audience.

But if one turns from it to a story like George Moore's "Home Sickness" in *The Untilled Field* one realizes that Moore's story does not need fire nor candlelight nor any audience other than oneself. It is the simple story of a New York barman who is sent back to Ireland to regain his health and falls in love with an Irish girl. He is hindered from settling down with her by a suspicion of his neighbors' timidity and the loutishness of the local priest. One day, haunted by the memory of frank and friendly discussions in America, he slips back to New York, and at the end of the story, whenever he thinks of Ireland he thinks of the girl he abandoned there to the loneliness and cowardice of her world, and his memories have a new poignancy. Contrast the cool and sympathetic intelligence of Moore's final paragraph with the schoolgirl high jinks of the passage from Somerville and Ross:

There is an unchanging, silent life within every man that none knows but himself, and his unchanging, silent life was his memory of Margaret Dirken. The bar-room was forgotten and all that concerned it and the things he saw most clearly were the green hill-side, and the bog lake and the rushes about it, and the greater lake in the distance, and behind it the blue line of wandering hills.

Here there is no contrivance, not so much as a single coincidence. The narrative line is merely a pattern: the pattern of human life as we have all experienced it—nostalgia and disillusionment and a fresh nostalgia sharpened by experience. It has the absolute purity of the short story as opposed to the tale, and it bears the same relationship to "Harrington's" that a song of Hugo Wolf's bears to "Du Lieber Augustin." You may like or dislike it—and my own attitude to the short story is somewhat ambivalent—but as a piece of artistic organization it is perfect. It represents an art form as elaborate as the sonnet, and—what is much more important to a student of the form—it points out the direction that the Irish short story would take. Though I suspect that for one copy of *The Untilled Field* you can find, you will find a hundred of *The Irish R.M.*, Irish literature has gone Moore's way, not Somerville and Ross's.

It is right that Moore should get the credit which at present goes to his unruly disciple Joyce, for though, as the work of the two men developed, it showed great differences—Moore giving way to his passion for polemic, Joyce to his for formal experiment—the early stories in *Dubliners* derive much from Moore.

So, I believe, do the stories of Liam O'Flaherty, though O'Flaherty might easily never have read

Moore. His novels, at least, suggest as much, but whereas in O'Flaherty's novels he makes mistakes that Moore could never have made, in his stories he avoids all the mistakes that Moore would certainly have made. If one wished to write a thesis to show that the novel was not an Irish form but that the short story was, one could do worse than take O'Flaherty for text. His subject is instinct, not judgment. "When O'Flaherty thinks, he's a goose, when he feels, he's a genius," is how George Russell, the poet, summed him up. His best stories deal with animals, and the nearer his characters approach to animals the happier he is in dealing with them. With his passion for polemic, Moore in "Home Sickness" could not ignore the fact that emigration is largely caused by the sheer boredom of an authoritarian religion. With his own natural innocence O'Flaherty in a story like "Going Into Exile" could ignore everything except the nature of exile itself—a state of things like love and death that we must all endure.

And one can easily imagine the sort of mess that George Moore would have made of O'Flaherty's "Fairy Goose," one of the great Irish short stories. It is the story of a feeble little goose whom the superstition of her owner turns into the divinity of an Irish village. She makes the fortune and turns the head of her owner until the parish priest decides to break up the cult, and the village louts stone the poor little goose to death. In essence, it is the whole history of religion, and it screams for a George Moore, an Anatole France, or a Norman Douglas, but because he is feeling rather than thinking, O'Flaherty never permits the shadow of a sneer to disturb the gravity of the theme. We laugh, all right, much louder than Moore or France or Douglas ever made us laugh—but at the same time we are moved, and eventually the impression left on our minds is something like that left by Turgenev's "Byezhin Prairie"—"the eternal silence of those infinite spaces terrifies me."

If I knew as much about American literature as I do about Irish literature, I feel I should probably be able to put my finger on Sherwood Anderson's *Winesburg, Ohio,* and say, "This is to America what *The Untilled Field* is to Ireland." The date itself—1919—is as significant as the date 1903 on the title page of Moore's book. Participation in the First World War had made Americans conscious for the first time since the Civil War that they were isolated, unique, and complacent; and the dissatisfaction it roused in them turned them into a generation of displaced persons, at home neither in America nor on the Continent. The year 1919 and Sherwood Anderson signaled the beginnings of a new self-consciousness; by 1920 Scott Fitzgerald was describing the return of the troops and the fresh complications this was creating, and within a couple of years Hemingway and Faulkner were sketching out the new literature.

When I said that I could think of no great storyteller who was not a great writer, I excluded Anderson, who did not really begin to write till he was in his forties. But few writers have had so clear a vision of what the short story could do. With absolute certainty he marked out his own submerged population—the lonely dreamers of the Middle West. Their loneliness is deeper and more tragic than that of

George Moore's priests or Joyce's clerks, perhaps because, like Anderson himself, they come of pioneering stock, confident, competent men and women who do not understand what it means to be beaten almost from birth. There is an interesting comparison to be drawn between Joyce's "Eveline" and Anderson's "Adventure." Both deal with sensitive women who for one reason or another have been left on the shelf. Eveline is waiting to go with the man she loves to Buenos Aires, but when the boat is on the point of departure she leaves him and runs home, beaten before she starts at all. Alice Hindman, who has waited hopelessly for the return of a man she loves, strips herself and runs out into the street one rainy night to offer herself to the first man she meets, but he turns out to be old and deaf and says nothing but "What? What say?" So Alice returns to the house, goes to bed, and "turning her face to the wall, began trying to face bravely the fact that many people must live and die alone, even in Winesburg." It is a terrible moment for the American when his clear-sighted optimism gives place to an equally clear-sighted despondency. Anderson's characters understand their own hopeless position so well that I sometimes find myself wondering whether they are not really examples of that passive suffering which Yeats maintained was no material for art.

Those two terrible words, "alone" and "lonely," ring out in almost every story in *Winesburg, Ohio,* and with them the word "hands"—hands reaching out for a human contact that is not there. Yet contact itself is the principal danger, for to marry is to submit to the standards of the submerged population, and for the married there is no hope but to pass on the dream of escape to their children. The danger is the theme of the beautiful story, "The Untold Lie," and of a later, inferior story, "The Contract." The hope transmitted to the children is the theme of Anderson's finest story, "Death." In this, George Willard's grandfather, distrusting his son-in-law, leaves his daughter eight hundred dollars to be "a great open door" to her when the time comes for her to escape. Elizabeth, defeated in her turn, has saved it to be "a great open door" to her son, George, and hidden it a week after her marriage in a wall at the foot of her bed, where at the end of the story it still lies, plastered up and forgotten.

It is from this remarkable little book that the modern American short story develops, and the Americans have handled the short story so wonderfully that one can say that it is a national art form. I have given one reason for the superiority of the American short story over all others that I know, but of course, there are several reasons, and one is that America is largely populated by submerged population groups. That peculiar American sweetness toward the stranger. —which exists side by side with American brutality toward everyone—is the sweetness of people whose own ancestors have been astray in an unfamiliar society and understand that a familiar society is the exception rather than the rule; that strangeness of behavior which is the very lifeblood of the short story is often an atavistic breaking out from some peculiar way of life, faraway and long ago.

One of the many stories of my American students which I remember better than I do my own is one written by a Jewish boy about a woman who kept an old junk shop in New York and whose son stole quarters and fifty-cent pieces from the till for his own amusements. One evening he comes home and finds the till broken into and his mother unconscious. She had been mugged by another Jew whom she recognized. But when her son tries to call the police she goes mad. "Isn't it bad enough for poor Mrs. Birnbaum she should have a son a dirty thief without my sending the police to her?" "After that," the story ends, "I gave up stealing from the till."

Oh, Jews, you say! But that story isn't merely Jewish any more than Saroyan's loveliest stories are merely Armenian, or, indeed, Katherine Anne Porter's stories merely Negro or Irish. It is a voice from other worlds, like that of the little copying clerk in Gogol's "Overcoat" crying, "I am your brother."

That, I fancy, is the importance of J. F. Powers' stories to me. It is not a racial one, though, judging by his name, Mr. Powers must be even more Irish than I am. The best of his stories deal with priests or would-be priests, intruders on a money society, though the money society has left the mark of its dirty paws on the Church to which they belong. Powers has discovered a genuine submerged population as disturbing as Saroyan's Armenians, Willa Cather's spoiled artists, and Anderson's spoiled romantics, and again, across the abyss that separates me from them I seem to hear the voice of Gogol's copying clerk, crying, "I am your brother."

But, at the time of writing, the most typical of modern American storytellers is J. D. Salinger. It is not only that he has developed the form itself as no one since Chekhov had done or that in his work it stands out as precisely what it is—the anti-novel. What makes him typical is that though his theme is still human loneliness the loneliness is specific instead of generalized.

True, he makes a bold bid for our sympathy by producing characters who are the product of a Jewish-Irish marriage—the loneliest combination of submerged populations one can imagine. But in spite of this he has no submerged population, no objectivization for the loneliness in himself that he externalizes: all his characters are Hamlets. This may account for his popularity among young people who always tend to regard themselves as Hamlets. Zachary Glass is a grown man and apparently a very successful figure in a highly competitive commercial occupation—television yet he is as isolated in his private world as any adolescent. Apparently, he doesn't get drunk and say silly things as some of us do, nor does he go home with the secretary to her apartment. One would like to know how he does it.

We can see the development in Salinger's work. In the most beautiful of the early stories—"For Esme, With Love and Squalor," a masterpiece if ever there was one—a conversation with a pert little English child saves the reason of an American soldier stationed abroad. In "A Splendid Day for Banana Fish" such a conversation does not save Seymour Glass from suicide. In "Franny" a girl on the verge of a nervous breakdown comes to a college match to meet the young man she is in love with and then cracks up in the women's lavatory and just recites, "Jesus, have mercy on me."

And already, in three stories we have run into serious critical difficulty. When "Franny" appeared college students and teachers split on the question of whether Franny was pregnant or not. This was not clumsiness on the part of the author, nor overcleverness on the part of readers. It was a real critical awareness on the part of the readers that somehow the story was insufficiently motivated—a point that is fully demonstrated by its sequel, "Zooey," in which Zachary Glass tries to deal with his sister's breakdown. For Zooey, like Franny, seems to have no animal existence. This was what the original readers were attempting to supply when they plumped for Franny's pregnancy. Pregnancy is a fact of animal life, and subconsciously they were aware that this was missing.

It is implied if not stated in "Franny" that she and her young man are lovers. At least they have been keeping company for a year and it had apparently not dawned on the young man that she was frigid. She is fastidious about animal food but there is no hint that she is repelled by animal contact. Franny, so far as I can see, is enduring a moral crisis without a morality. Her "Jesus" is completely disembodied, unrelated to any spiritual inadequacy in herself and to any possible roots this might have in her animal nature.

This becomes clearer in the long and beautifully composed sequel. Zooey is twenty-eight; he is a successful actor in a television performance that he despises. At his age he is presumably not sexually innocent. Like Franny and their dead brother, Seymour, he is a God-seeker, yet never once are we told that his quest for ultimate reality affects his sexual life or his attitude to his work. Spiritual dissatisfaction does not drive him to leave his job and take up something that might satisfy him spiritually.

My only doubt about the Glass family is that they seem to me already perfect, and what is perfect can only fade.

We have been told that the novel is dead, and I am sure that someone has said as much for the short story. I suspect that the announcement may prove a little premature, and I should be much readier to listen to an argument that poetry and the theater were dead. I should not be too enthusiastic about that either, but I should be prepared to admit that since they are both primitive arts there would be some sort of case to answer. But the novel and the short story are drastic adaptations of a primitive art form to modern conditions—to printing, science, and individual religion—and I see no possibility of or reason for their supersession except in a general supersession of all culture by mass civilization. I suppose if this takes place, we shall all have to go into monasteries, or—if mass civilization forbids—into catacombs and caves, but even there, I suspect, more than one worshiper will be found clutching a tattered copy of *Pride and Prejudice* or *The Short Stories of Anton Chekhov.*

July 21, 1962

1. Hamlet and Quixote

A SPORTSMAN'S SKETCHES may well be the greatest book of short stories ever written. Nobody, at the time that it was written, knew quite how great it was, or what influence it was to have in the creation of a new art form. It attracted ambiguous notoriety because of its supposed effect in the campaign for the emancipation of serfs in Russia, but this has nothing to do with its merits as a book. It is not propaganda but fiction—that is to say, it is not a solution in artistic terms of any social problem but a solution of its creator's own conflict. That point is made in the very first story, "Khor and Kalinitch."

As a man, Turgenev had one personal problem which he illustrates endlessly in his work. He felt that he was himself a weak, ineffectual figure—which he wasn't—and had a great admiration for practical men. He dealt with this in a famous critical essay on Hamlet and Don Quixote in which he treated himself as Hamlet and sang the praises of Quixote, the madman who does the world's work while Hamlet, the

46

thinker, merely sits back and monologizes. In *The Mirror in the Roadway* I tried to analyze one novel of Turgenev's—*On the Eve*—and show the difficulties in which he involved himself by trying to impose objective reality on this subjective pattern. The model for the hero of *On the Eve*, Insarov, was a poet, but Turgenev could not possibly believe in a man of action who also wrote poetry, so Insarov in the novel is presumed to be devoid of any taste for literature. But when it came down to novel writing, Turgenev found it equally impossible to portray a man who was absolutely devoid of poetry, so when we first meet Insarov, he is translating Bulgarian songs and chronicles. Then, realizing what he is doing, Turgenev tries to cover up his tracks by making someone say that the translations are not very good. And yet the old passion breaks out, and Insarov cries to his sweetheart, Elena: "We have such wonderful songs! As good as the Serbian. But just wait. I'll translate one of them for you." This is something I often say myself about eighth-century Irish poetry, and I believe that I was justified in saying that though it may be the language of a man who is not himself a poet, it is emphatically not the language of one who has no taste for poetry. And yet, twenty pages later, Elena tells us that neither she nor Insarov cares for poetry!

"Khor and Kalinitch" is a perfect example of the same dilemma. Khor is a coarse, powerful, practical intelligence, who from nothing creates a family of fine sons and a little fortune; Kalinitch is a dreamer who plays the balalaika. Kalinitch can read, Khor cannot. As a man, Turgenev simply could not see that a practical intelligence like Khor's had anything at all to learn from books. And yet, whenever he came to deal with this personal conflict, Turgenev—one of the subtlest intelligences in the history of literature—betrayed himself like a schoolboy. In real life there *was* a Khor, and Turgenev admired Khor and sent him a copy of the story, *which Khor proudly read to all his visitors.* In other words, when he came to deal with his own personal problem, Turgenev faked his psychology.

Technically, the story is interesting principally because episodic interest is almost entirely suppressed. We see Poliutin, the idiotic owner of both Khor and Kalinitch, and realize that, though Kalinitch permits himself to be exploited by his master, Khor is more than a match for him. The device which Turgenev uses instead of the old-fashioned narrative is antithesis—the contrast between the dreamer and the practical man—and however that device may have been abused by later writers, Turgenev always uses it with artistry. It merely means that as narrative is abandoned the storyteller turns to the devices of the prose writer pure and simple—dramatic irony and antithesis.

The second story, "Yermolai and the Miller's Wife," is vastly more interesting. Arina, a slave girl taken in as maid by the wife of a wealthy landowner, falls in love with a footman called Petrushka and wishes to marry him; but her mistress—"an angel in human form" as her husband, the landowner says—prefers her maids unmarried, so when Arina, that monster of ingratitude, starts a baby, the footman is sent to the army and a crusty old miller buys Arina's freedom and marries her. In her loneliness and misery

Arina carries on a love affair with a waster called Yermolai who is a sort of wild man of the woods.

Now, once more, Turgenev's technique has become so standardized that it eludes our attention. He telescopes the whole action into the events of a single night. He tells of the narrator's night out hunting with Yermolai, of the miller's churlishness when the two men seek a shelter, of the escape of the miller's wife to talk for a few minutes with Yermolai; and finally the narrator remembers the sad tale of ingratitude that had been told him by Arina's owner, Mr. Zverkov, husband of the "angel in human form." It ends with the two really important characters, Arina and Petrushka, dismissed in a few lines of casual conversation between the narrator and Yermolai.

"And do you know the footman, Petrushka?"
"You mean Peter Vasilyevitch? Of course I knew him."
"Where is he now?"
"He was sent for a soldier."
We were silent for a while.
"She doesn't seem well?" I asked Yermolai at last.
"I should think not! Tomorrow, I say, we shall have some sport."

Here we have the essence of the modern short story, Turgenev's marvelous development of Gogol's discovery. Again I would repeat that the technical device has been so abused by later writers that it does not impress us as it must have impressed Turgenev's contemporaries. The telescoping of a whole life story into the experiences and comments of a couple of supernumeraries is a device that has been so overworked that my own inclination would be to scrap it and tell the story as I have told it here in chronological order, without frills and flourishes. I suspect that that is exactly how the mature Turgenev would have told it. But in its historical context one can admire the audacious way in which the story is "thrown away" in the theatrical sense, how all the human agony emerges only at moments from that maze of irrelevance, as though it were the very voice of the submerged population. And yet this was also a favorite device of Robert Browning, and one can read "Yermolai and the Miller's Wife" side by side with "My Last Duchess" and notice how the two throw light on one another, even to the deliberate anticlimax at the end of each. "Tomorrow, I say, we shall have some sport" is almost echoed in

> Nay, we'll go
> Together down, sir! Notice Neptune, though,
> Taming a seahorse, thought a rarity
> Which Claus of Innsbruck cast in bronze for me.

The characters themselves seem to echo one another: Arina, the Duchess; Petrushka, Fra Pandolf; and Mr. Zverkov, the Duke—the cold egocentric by whom all this innocent love and gentleness is smothered.

But there are even more characteristic stories than these, like the two Henry James admired so much—"The Singers" and "Byezhin Prairie." "The Singers" describes a singing contest in a country tavern, "Byezhin Prairie" a group of four boys, grazing their horses at night on a river bank in a prairie, where they pass their time telling ghost stories. At least, that, on the surface, is all they purport to describe, but, in fact, as the former story really describes the power of art to add meaning to a meaningless world, the latter deals with the meaninglessness of life itself and the terror of the human soul alone with Nature and the night.

An English or American editor of Turgenev's day would have been happier with these two pieces than with the former pair, for he would have had no difficulty in finding a name for them. He would have recognized them immediately as essays, such as Hazlitt might have written, and published them under the title of "Country Songs" or "Ghost Stories." What he would not have understood is our describing them as "stories," for stories, to him, would have meant narratives in which the episodic interest was predominant, and Turgenev has simply removed the episodic interest and replaced it with the static quality of an essay or a poem. For one moment at the end of "Byezhin Prairie" he allows the episodic interest to return when Paul, the manliest of the four boys, believes he hears the voice of a drowned comrade calling him from the depths of the river, but even this Turgenev deliberately dispels in the final paragraph when he tells us what Paul's real fate was.

Sad to say, I must add that in that year Pavlusha met his end. He was not drowned; he was killed by a fall from his horse. Pity! He was a splendid fellow.

The anticlimax here is a perfect example of Turgenev's supreme artistry. "He was not drowned; he was killed by a fall from his horse." Gogol could have used these local ghost stories quite as well as Turgenev did, but he could never have resisted the opportunity of adding the final touch that would send the shiver down our spine. This was not the sort of shiver that Turgenev wanted—the shudder of children sitting over the fire on a winter night, thinking of ghosts and banshees while the wind cries about the little cottage—but that of the grown man before the mystery of human life.

In his later stories Turgenev returned to the earlier form he had used—that of the *nouvelle*. Because we so badly need a term for it we should perhaps ignore the unfortunate connotations of the word and simply say "novelette" to describe the short novel or the long short story. The difference between the two forms is simple enough to perceive but much more difficult to describe, and a similar difficulty arises when we come to deal with the difference between the novelette and the novel.

Now, "Yermolai and the Miller's Wife" is a short story—a *conte* if you can stand the French term. That is to say, the whole narrative has been concentrated into one single episode, by telescoping the events of several years into those of one night with the aid of the flashback and of indirect narration. Except when it is used by a very scrupulous artist, this is an exceedingly dangerous device, because not only does the combination of exposition and development confuse and weary the reader, but the whole may be something quite different from the sum of the parts—as in one of Maupassant's stories which I shall have to discuss where, as a result of the treatment, a very moving little story turns into an unseemly farce. As I have said, if I had had to write the story of "Yermolai and the Miller's Wife" I should have preferred the form of the novelette, begun at the beginning with

Arina, described her experiences with Mrs. Zverkov, that "angel in human form," traced the desperation that led to her love affair with Petrushka, and then tried to describe how her marriage to an inhuman old man turned her into the casual mistress of a waster like Yermolai.

But I should at the same time have had to ask myself whether the story could be told in this way at all. The advantage of the *conte* form is that everything is over and done with before the story proper begins. Whatever sort of people Arina and Petrushka were in real life, whatever sort of fight they put up against their destiny, their destiny had already been decided, and that is the subject of Turgenev's story. If I take their characters into account I must ask myself whether some weakness in them could not have accounted for their destiny, and whether the details of their fight against destiny are of sufficient interest to justify me in describing them. The question is whether by particularizing I shall not distract attention from the brutal egocentricity which would have condemned them to frustration and loneliness anyhow—whether "My Last Duchess" could ever have been told from the point of view of the Duchess. If I tried to write the story in this way, I should already be one step on the road to the novel.

But that is the way Turgenev chose to write stories for the rest of his life, and though his collected novelettes might not make a book as beautiful as *A Sportsman's Sketches,* it would contain three masterpieces—"The Watch," "Punin and Baburin," and "Old Portraits."

Why I discuss these as stories rather than as novels

illustrates the difficulty of defining the difference between the novelette and the novel. The problem is made worse by the attitude of publishers and public. In Victorian England a novel was believed to be a story in three volumes and two hundred thousand words. In our own day, when people's patience is less and publishing costs are higher, the accepted length is eighty thousand words, and any publisher will tell you that the public won't look at anything longer. Mr. E. M. Forster, who knows more about it than any of us, says, "We may perhaps go so far as to add that the extent should not be less than fifty thousand words." Georges Simenon's novels, which the French public accepts as novels, are all in about thirty thousand words, but when they are translated into English they are usually published in pairs to make them look more like real novels. What I mean by this is that a novel is not only a literary form; it is also a convention, and in discussing the form we should beware of letting the convention intrude on the argument.

Turgenev's novels are not long, and nearly always fail to reach the sacred eighty thousand, which may be why Mr. Forster lowered his sights, since it would be absurd if one of the greatest of all novelists were to be excluded by definition. Turgenev's novelettes are rarely short and they do not easily fit into an anthology of short stories. But I think I am right in saying that his novels *are* novels and his novelettes short stories, whatever the difficulty about describing the difference. Dmitry Mirsky, who was clearly troubled by this particular problem, made a neat distinction when he pointed out that the novelettes do not contain the long and often tiresome conversations about general ideas that the Russian public expected from a "serious" novelist. Before reading Mirsky, I had written that the difference was that the characters in the novclettes, unlike the characters in the novels, were not intended to have general significance, which may be only another way of saying the same thing, though, if this is so, I think it a more accurate one. After all, Chekhov, who was a storyteller pure and simple, did have a tendency to introduce those tedious discussions on general ideas into his stories, but this does not make them into novels. Even "The Duel," which is quite as long as many novels are, is full of these discussions, but it is still recognizably a short story. Perhaps, at the same time, I belabor the point, because it fits in with my own view of the difference between novel and story as one between characters regarded as representative figures and characters regarded as outcasts, lonely individuals.

That is how I would state the difference between a novel like *Fathers and Sons* and a magnificent novelette like "Punin and Baburin." In both, Turgenev made use of the prototypes we found in "Khor and Kalinitch" and *On the Eve*. Each story represents the conflict between the man of action and the dreamer—Quixote and Hamlet, Turgenev would have said. In the short story Baburin is the man of action, the illegitimate son of a good family who has protected and sheltered a poor old poetaster, Punin. He is employed for a time as clerk by a woman described as the narrator's grandmother, who is really Turgenev's own mother. She sends into exile a slave of hers who did not take off his cap to her with sufficient alacrity.

(Turgenev used to show visitors the window at which his mother sat when her poor victims came to pay their respects before leaving for the army or exile.) Baburin protests and is dismissed.

The next episode occurs seven years later. Baburin has picked up another lame duck, an orphan girl of good family whom he proposes to marry, Musa Pavlovna, but Musa becomes the mistress of a worthless aristocratic friend of the narrator's instead. Twelve years later, the narrator meets Baburin and Musa Pavlovna again. Punin has died, and Musa, cast off by her lover, has again been rescued by Baburin, who has married her. Baburin is sent to Siberia as a political prisoner, and Musa follows him; and when he dies there, she continues his work for the revolution, a dedicated woman but with the springs of joy dried up inside her.

Now, this wonderful story, one of the great masterpieces of fiction, could easily have been the subject of a full-length novel, but as Turgenev treats it, it never even begins to be a novel. You may say with Mirsky that this is because it is not discursive in the usual way of a Russian novel. I would urge my own suggestion that it is not a novel because it is not generalized in the manner of a novel. The two characters of the title represent the fundamental conflict in Turgenev, between action and poetry, but neither of them is a character with whom the reader could possibly identify himself. They are too specialized, too eccentric, too—I should almost say—grotesque. The reader's impression is that of the narrator.

Baburin aroused in me a feeling of hostility with which there was, however, in a short time, mingled something akin to respect. And wasn't I afraid of him! I never got over being afraid of him even when the sharp severity of his manner with me at first had quite disappeared. It is needless to say that of Punin I had no fear; I did not even respect him; I looked upon him not to put too fine a point on it—as a buffoon; but I loved him with my whole soul.

Baburin is one of the greatest bits of character drawing in literature, and when I finally met in real life a man who resembled him, I found myself with precisely the feelings that Turgenev has so wonderfully described. Respect, yes, admiration, perhaps, but identification with him—impossible! One merely wondered whether his fate under any government would not have been equally gloomy.

In an essay on "Turgenev and the Life-Giving Drop," Mr. Edmund Wilson has analyzed another beautiful novelette, "The Watch," and his analysis, brilliant as it is, not only illustrates the weakness of a certain type of American criticism but emphasizes the sort of misunderstanding that occurs when a great critic, accustomed to the art of the novel, deals with the short story. Mr. Wilson writes:

In this ingenious parable, the narrator is given a watch by his godfather, a corrupt official who has lost his job but who still always powders his hair. . . . He is delighted by the present at first, but a cousin, whose father has been sent to Siberia, for "agitational activities and Jacobin views," carefully examines the watch, declares that it is old and no good and learning that it was given by the boy by his godfather, tells him that he should accept no gifts from such a man. The narrator worships the cousin, and the rest of the story consists of his efforts to get rid of the watch by burying it or giving it away. But he always—under pressure of his family or of his own inextinguishable pride in it—is compelled to get it back again. What does this watch represent?

The antiquated social system? The corruption of old Russia? The father and the godfather are crooks; the watch, though the boy does not realize it, has evidently been stolen. It is only at last expelled from their lives when the tough-minded Jacobin hurls it into the river at the cost of falling in himself and of almost getting drowned.

It may well be that Mr. Wilson has really pierced to the heart of Turgenev's intention in this adorable little novelette—a lightweight beside "Punin and Baburin" but with a lovely gaiety which is too rare in Turgenev. I hope he hasn't, because I shouldn't like to think that something which seems to move only from within is really being moved from outside by the desire to teach a lesson. I do not think he has, for the first thing the critic has to notice is that once again we have the Quixote-Hamlet grouping in the dumb, decent elder boy, David, and the younger, more poetic, Alexey, who tells the story. As usual in Turgenev it is Hamlet who is the dependent. The story tells of David's love for an underdog—little Raissa, whose father has had a stroke that results in verbal confusions in his speech, and whose younger sister is deaf and dumb. Through David's loving eyes we see Raissa's gallant effort at providing for her two helpless relatives, and this magical love story—with its overtones of personal grief that the narrator, who really loves David and admires his manliness and courage, is himself a Hamlet who vacillates over every trifling decision—is told with impudent dexterity in terms of a watch, a cheap watch, something so commonplace that it seems impossible that it could have ever formed a link between such complex characters. As for Mr. Wilson's expulsion of the watch from the characters' lives, he ignores the fact that the narrator ends his story with "But in a secret drawer of my writing table is preserved an old silver watch with a rose on its face; I bought it of a Jew peddler, being struck with its resemblance to the watch which had once been presented to me by my godfather. From time to time, when I am alone, and not expecting anyone, I take it out of its box, and as I gaze at it, I recall the days of my youth and the comrade of those days, which have vanished beyond recall."

Is it really "the antiquated social system" that the narrator is preserving in the drawer of his table? Is it possible that this can be "the corruption of old Russia" over which he lingers? Surely not! Turgenev's lesson, insofar as one can imagine him teaching anything at all, is that of those much-caricatured and underrated lines:

> Be good, sweet child, and let who will be clever;
> Do noble things, not dream them, all day long;
> And so make life, death and that vast Forever
> One grand sweet song.

"Old Portraits" is probably Turgenev's greatest story; indeed, if I were to answer so foolish a question as "which is the greatest story in the world?" I should probably light on this. It is not episodic, but neither is it exactly a short story in the manner of those in *A Sportsman's Sketches*. It is written casually in the manner of reminiscence, and only careful reading will show how carefully it is constructed. Its subject is the eighteenth century, which Turgenev loved, and it is represented through the characters of an old couple who illustrate everything that Turgenev thought wonderful in that wonderful century. They

are described lightly, gaily, and one settles down to
enjoy another tale like Gogol's "Old-Fashioned Land-
owners" with its delightful Bob and Joan portraits of
an ingenuous old couple. Then the old man dies, and
suddenly the whole mood of the story deepens in that
extraordinary scene which no other writer of fiction
in the world could have written. The little domestic
jokes of the first section are repeated but with an almost unearthly poignancy.

"Alexis!" she cried suddenly, "don't frighten me, don't
shut your eyes! Are you in pain?" The old man looked at
his wife: "No, no pain . . . but it's difficult . . . difficult to
breathe." Then after a brief silence: "Malania," he said,
"so life has slipped by—and do you remember when we
were married . . . what a couple we were?" "Yes, we were,
my handsome, charming Alexis!" The old man was silent
again. "Malania, my dear, shall we meet again in the next
world?" "I will pray God for it, Alexis," and the old woman
burst into tears. "Come, don't cry, silly; maybe the Lord
God will make us young again then—and again we shall be
a fine pair!" "He will make us young, Alexis!" "With the
Lord all things are possible," observed Alexey Sergeitch.
"He worketh great marvels!—maybe He will make you
sensible. . . . There, my love, I was joking; come, let me
kiss your hand." "And I yours." And the two old people
kissed each other's hands simultaneously.

Alexey Sergeitch began to grow quieter and to sink into
forgetfulness. Malania Pavlovna watched him tenderly,
brushing the tears off her eyelashes with her finger-tips. For
two hours she continued sitting there. "Is he asleep?" the
old woman with her talent for praying inquired in a
whisper, peeping in behind Irinarkh, who, immovable as a
post, stood in the doorway, gazing intently at his expiring
master. "He is asleep," Malania Pavlovna answered also in
a whisper. And suddenly Alexey Sergeitch opened his eyes.
"My faithful companion," he faltered, "my honoured wife,

I would bow down at your little feet for all your love and faithfulness—but how to get up? Let me sign you with the cross." Malania Pavlovna moved closer, bent down. . . . But the hand he had raised fell back powerless on the quilt, and a few moments later Alexey Sergeitch was no more.

There is an extraordinary passage in the Goncourt *Journals* in which the group of Turgenev's French friends, Flaubert and the other writers of his group, discussed the fact that none of them had ever been in love, and then listened in fascination as Turgenev told them how he had been in love, with a slave girl. They thought it extraordinary. They might not have thought it quite so extraordinary if they had known "Old Portraits."

And then, suddenly, curtly, Turgenev slips into what appears to be a complete digression about a coachman of the old man, a serf of uncertain status who had finally to be returned to his legal owner and who threatened to kill him if he were. No one pays any attention to the little joker's threats till one day he does kill his master and is sent to the mines to spend the rest of his days there. "They were good old times, but enough of them!" the story ends. It is not only the whole eighteenth century that is expressed in this miraculous story, but the whole of Turgenev as well, and there are few writers who had as much of the essential stuff of humanity in them as Turgenev.

2. Country Matters

A E. COPPARD used to say that if ever he edited
. an anthology of short stories he would have
an easy job because half the book would be by Chekhov and the other half by Maupassant. That was how
Maupassant's reputation stood when Coppard was
young, though I doubt if it is how it stands now.

Gustave Flaubert, who was the intimate friend of
Maupassant's uncle, acted as literary adviser to the
nephew and gave him good advice that Maupassant
recorded later in the introduction to *Pierre et Jean*.
The essence of it is in the last sentence, which was
passed on to me in my own youth by another distinguished older writer: "By a single word make me see
wherein one cab horse differs from fifty others before
or behind it." Later, Liam O'Flaherty said to me, "If
you can describe a hen crossing a road you are a real
writer." It never did me the least bit of good, and to
this day I couldn't describe a cab horse or a hen.

Just before his death Flaubert was able to hail
Maupassant's story "Boule de Suif" as a masterpiece,

which it is. It is a novelette about a coachload of
French people making a journey during the German
occupation after the war of 1870. One of the travelers
is a prostitute, "Boule de Suif" or "Roly-Poly," and
she has had forethought enough to provide herself
with provisions for the journey, so that her fellow
travelers who have neglected this precaution, having
first snubbed her because of her profession, are forced
into common politeness by simple greed. The coach
is stopped by the Germans who will not allow the
party to proceed till the prostitute obliges the German
officer. The prostitute, being a true patriot, refuses.

Now, this is all very well, but it holds up her fellow travelers, and they are compelled to use powerful
arguments on the silly girl to induce her to yield.
The most powerful, because it has the blessing of the
Church, is that of the Sister of Mercy who gives it as
her opinion that "an action blamable in itself is often
rendered meritorious by the impulse which inspires
it," a good Christian principle which Yeats turned
into admirable verse:

> the Light of Lights
> Looks always on the motive, not the deed,
> The Shadow of Shadows on the deed alone.

With the highest of motives, Boule de Suif, like
Father Gaucher in Daudet's story and Countess Cathleen in Yeats's play, sacrifices her soul in the interest
of the community, but suddenly the community turns
from the Light of Lights to the Shadow of Shadows
and, having made use of her, casts her aside. As the
coach proceeds, her fellow travelers treat the poor girl
with open contempt. *This* time they have not forgotten their provisions while she in her abasement

has, and they shamelessly eat in front of her while, hungry and humiliated, she sits weeping in their midst. A masterpiece without doubt, but definitely not a pleasant one; not one that makes you think better of yourself or your fellow men.

And yet it is a masterpiece. Even in this, his first published story, Maupassant comes before us equipped with his own subject—the submerged sexual population of nineteenth-century Europe. Others had treated it before him, undoubtedly, but he was the man who put his seal on it, who identified himself publicly with the prostitutes, the girls with illegitimate children, the children themselves. Until he established them as a real theme, they had been generally treated as a dirty joke, a joke of the music halls and the comic papers, which knew the truth behind the brassy hypocrisy of the age; but even when one turns on Maupassant for perpetuating the dirty joke, as he so often did, one turns on him for denying his own vision of life, the truth that he came into the world to expound. His life itself may be considered an allegory, for scarcely had he attained fame than he was destroyed by the disease that ravaged the whole submerged population he wrote about. And that, as Arnold says, is the tragedy of the true poet—"we become what we sing."

This was Maupassant's subject—his obsession, if you will—and his greatest stories all deal with it. "The Tellier House," for instance, which seems to me his real masterpiece and far, far superior to "Boule de Suif," deals with a brothel in Fécamp—the only brothel in the town. The respectable citizens who meet there at night are horrified when they find the brothel

closed and a notice that reads "Closed Because of
First Communion." (That, I suspect, was the actual
spark that set fire to the storyteller's imagination.) It
emerges that the Madam, attending the First Communion of her niece in a country village, has thought
it better to bring her staff of five with her, to keep
them out of harm's way, and these five women become the sensation of the village. The beauty of the
countryside and of the First Communion service, reminding them of their youth and innocence, appeals
to the overemotional characters of the prostitutes,
who give an edifying exhibition of tearful devotion,
and the parish priest, as innocent as the youngest of
his communicants, delivers a little speech in praise of
their faith and piety. The story ends with their return
to Fécamp and the relief and enthusiasm of their customers there. Madam and girls are equally pleased to
be home, for everyone feels that he or she has had a
narrow escape from virtue. The public repudiation of
the victim in "Boule de Suif" is something I don't
recognize—or hope I don't recognize—but the momentary relief from the necessity for being good is a feeling that I suspect most decent men and women have
shared.

It is overdone, of course; Maupassant could never
resist overdoing an effect. The priest's address, like
the Sister of Mercy's theology in "Boule de Suif," be-
labors a point that has been made over and over again
and forces a dull student of the short story like myself
to ask what has happened to the cab horse. I am the
last person on earth who should be asked to identify
the cab horse but I long for some slight indication
that would enable me to identify the priest or the

nun. Still, "The Tellier House" is a great and brilliant work of art, like the Toulose-Lautrec pictures
of the brothel that it so much resembles.

"The Tellier House," "Boule de Suif," and the
beautiful "Story of a Farm Girl" all belong to a tiny
group of stories written under the direct influence of
Flaubert and in an approximation to Flaubert's manner, with a wealth of detail—novelist's detail—which
I sometimes find overpowering, as in the opening
paragraphs of "Boule de Suif," which would be very
pleasant in a novel of eighty thousand words. But
shortly after Flaubert's death Maupassant began to
write regularly for the weekly papers in a manner in
which style is sacrificed to narrative. As narrative
may be itself a form of style, it might be more accurate to say that style is sacrificed to anecdote.

Now, though I find the style of the early stories
overelaborate, I am much more repelled by the
skimpiness of the later ones. If I have to choose between too much and too little I prefer too much.
Even Mme. de Maupassant, who was no great shakes
as a literary critic, complained to her son that he
started his stories too soon, without sufficient preparation, and this seems to me perfectly true. Maupassant
again and again makes the point of his story without
convincing me that the characters through whom he
makes it ever existed. A work of art, like a philosophical discussion, is not only something more than the
point; it is by its very nature different from the point.
The point of a short story belongs to the basic anecdote—the brothel closed "Because of First Communion"—and as far as the literary critic is concerned
had better be smothered at birth. You do not exhaust

"The Tellier House" when you have made the point that the most pious people at the First Communion service are prostitutes. You don't even begin to touch it, because the surface of a great short story is like a sponge; it sucks up hundreds of impressions that have nothing whatever to do with the anecdote.

This may be the reason why none of the later stories of Maupassant make the same profound impression on me that "The Tellier House" does. At the same time, there is a whole group of stories which have the same sort of appeal for me. They are all stories that deal with Maupassant's obsession; with the submerged population of whom he made himself the spokesman. Take for instance a group of stories such as "In the Wood," "Indiscretion," and "A Country Excursion," all of which have something like a common theme. In "A Country Excursion," mother and daughter, out for the day with papa and the girl's intended, are seduced by two young oarsmen. A year later, when one of the oarsmen returns to the spot he finds the girl there with her boring husband. In "In the Wood," a virtuous girl goes out on a double date. Her friend and the friend's young man go deeper into the wood for serious lovemaking, but when her companion tries the same thing on the girl she fights him off. They are married and live together in a reasonable way, but years later, when they are old and weary of the business of living, the wife brings the husband back to the wood where he had tried to seduce her and forces him to make love to her. They are arrested for indecent behavior, and the wife defends herself before the Mayor, a sensible man who dismisses the case. In "Indiscretion," a young wife who is happily married but realizes that love is slipping from her in the routine and responsibility of married life makes her husband bring her to a low café where he had already brought many of his mistresses and pretend that they are not married, that in fact she is deceiving her husband even though it is only with himself. As they dine she makes him tell her of the other women he had brought there, throws her arms about his neck, and says dreamily, "Yes, it must be very amusing all the same."

You don't have to be a literary critic to see that like every other writer, either when he has got tired and begun repeating himself or when he is at the top of his power and can only repeat himself, Maupassant is writing the same story again and again. Undoubtedly the best version is also the earliest, for in "A Country Excursion" there is not only the "point," there is also the beauty of the river and woods and the bird's song which divert us from the point. "In the Wood" is ruined—at least for me—by the comic arrest and trial of the elderly couple for indecent behavior. Maupassant had enough psychological understanding to realize that a woman who was in fact compensating for what she felt to be the lack of romance in her earlier life would have died rather than admit it: the arrest is merely one of the slapstick devices he used to make the point more clear to the tired businessman and his frustrated wife. But the point is not a mean one; there may be weariness in the making of it but there was no weariness in its apprehension. The inspiration is there all the time in the three stories—the apprehension in all women, even in good and virtuous women, of what they have missed in life, the warmth and excitement of animal passion among the submerged population which they know only at a distance or in flashes.

One night in a Dublin street I watched an extraordinary scene between a tramp and a prostitute whose sad little affair had broken up—his hope of a home, hers of a husband. Bit by bit she stripped off the few garments he had bought for her, threw them at his feet, and stood in the cold night air shivering. Suddenly I looked around and saw a beautiful girl who was also watching the scene and realized that she was easily the most interesting figure in the little group. On her face was a look that I can describe only as one of exaltation. Maupassant would have followed that girl to her home.

Maupassant is equally good when it comes to girls with illegitimate children and the children themselves. "Simon's Daddy"—one of his earliest and loveliest stories—describes a little illegitimate boy driven to the verge of suicide by his schoolmates' taunts that he has no daddy. He is saved from drowning himself by the village blacksmith who, understanding the child's feeling of inadequacy, agrees to become his daddy. This works well enough until the other children recognize that the blacksmith is not the husband of Simon's mother and begin to persecute him again. Once more Simon goes with his troubles to the blacksmith who, to make a good job of it, marries the mother. It is a lovely story, sentimental if you like, but expressing—as Maupassant was only too often afraid to do—his real sympathy with his own submerged population.

"There are things one doesn't tell everyone, one doesn't tell a lawyer or a priest. Everybody does them and everybody knows about them, but they aren't mentioned, except when it can't be avoided." Those lines of the dying father in "The Hautots, Father and Son" express Maupassant's obsession—and his problem—and because of it he writes another story that has haunted me ever since I first read it. Old Hautot has been the lover of a poor girl who has had a child by him. On his deathbed he confesses it to his son and asks the boy to see her and provide for her. Young Hautot, a devoted son, does so and she becomes his mistress in turn—the ugliest theme a writer could imagine, but because Maupassant was inspired by it, it turns into a beautiful story.

And whenever he permitted the inspiration to take control he wrote beautifully, as in a late story like "Yvette" about a prostitute's daughter who is forced to realize that she must become a prostitute herself, and "Mouche" which has always had an appeal for me second only to that of "The Tellier House." It is about a little guttersnipe who attaches herself to five young oarsmen who frequent the Seine (the oarsmen of "A County Excursion") and becomes the mistress of one after the other until when she does become pregnant nobody has the least idea who the father may be. Undaunted, the five young men agree to adopt the baby communally. Then Mouche has a miscarriage and is inconsolable for the baby who would have represented to her all its five possible fathers until the young men console her by promising

that they will make her another. How can one morally
defend such an impossible theme? And yet in its wild
and lonely defiance of every accepted standard of
morality, "Mouche" is a little masterpiece in its own
right. For an elderly romantic it is all very, very
difficult.

Nevertheless, Maupassant's stories are *not* satisfactory. One has to compare him with Chekhov since
there is no one else to compare him with and he
suffers by the comparison. He suffers by comparison
even with Turgenev who was only a part-time storyteller. Someone like me whose French is indifferent
may wonder if he has not been mistranslated and long
to be able to read the Isaac Babel translation into
Russian which Babel describes in one of his stories.
The stories were translated mainly for elderly gentlemen who felt the need of a little extra sexual stimula-
tion, and Maupassant's American biographer, Francis
Steegmuller, has revealed the astonishing fact that
sixty-five of his stories which have circulated in America are not by Maupassant at all.

But this in itself is part of the thing that makes his
work so unsatisfactory. His inspiration is sexual, and
sex is a dangerous source of inspiration, for it so
easily becomes ambivalent, and stories and novels
that in their conception were a passionate protest
against the exploitation and degradation of sex easily
become merely another way of exploiting and degrad-
ing it. A man who chooses sex as his inspiration has
inherited a brothel; he may, of course, use it to make
the lives of his staff happier and better, but there is
always the possibility that he will use them for his

own profit and pleasure. Was there ever a publican with sense who did not realize the danger of drinking himself out of his business?

For a great part of his life, that is exactly what Maupassant was doing. He was both an inspired artist and a weak and very common man. After Flaubert's death he was never quite certain which part of himself he should present, and with what Mr. Steegmuller calls his "increasing worldliness"—his duchesses, his yacht, and his balloon trips—it was the common side of him that most often appeared. It is a question I find it hard to be censorious about. It is not the loss of his business that worries the sensible publican but the degradation which he knows must accompany it. How, if one is not one of the exploited, does one describe them without being one of the exploiters? Mauriac—or was it Maritain?—said the last word on obscenity in literature when he said that one may deal with anything but "one must purify the source." In Maupassant the source is never pure, and as he grew older it became more contaminated. The contamination comes through in the hysterical giggle, the sudden realization that this is not only a moving story but one that can raise a laugh when the women have left the room, or even before it if the women are of the same stuff as the men. Burns, the Puritan anti-Puritan, knew the real danger of promiscuity for the literary man:

> But och, it hardens all within
> And petrifies the feelings.

But even Burns, for all his self-knowledge, never understood the depths to which a writer could sink.

It is not only the hardening of the feelings, it is
not only the guffaw that follows the dirty story told
after dinner. It is the perversion of the creative faculty until it becomes destructive and the sexual act
itself turns into a form of murder. Anyone whom a
sense of social duty has compelled to listen to a real
pathological teller of indecent stories knows exactly
what hell opened to sinners is like.

That element of perversion was there in Maupassant from the beginning. What is really wrong with
"Boule de Suif" is not that it is overwritten or cyni-
cal, it is that it is not at all what it appears to be; not
another version of "Father Gaucher's Elixir" or
Countess Cathleen—the story of someone who sacrifices himself in the interest of the community—but the
story of a woman who has sexual relations with a man
whom it is her duty to kill. Murder has been replaced
by coition, and is, from her point of view and Maupassant's, an act of perversion. Love and death, the
creative and the destructive instincts, have switched
places.

That situation is made much clearer in another
story, "Mademoiselle Fifi," which is so like "Boule de
Suif" that—as Mr. Steegmuller points out—the people
who were making the film of one had merely to link
the other with it to produce a harmonious story. In
"Mademoiselle Fifi," a group of German officers who
are brutes and sadists to a man are billeted in a French
château, which they proceed to wreck. They decide
to bring out a party of prostitutes from Rouen to
spend the night. The five girls arrive, and Rachel, a
young Jewess, is allotted to the frail and vicious Marquis Wilhelm von Eyrick, known to his comrades as

"Mademoiselle Fifi." The Marquis is a sadist: in kissing Rachel he blows smoke into her face and later bites her till the blood flows. The Germans toast their victories over France and French women, and Rachel, outraged, says, "I am not a woman; I am a whore, and that is all that Prussians deserve." The Marquis strikes her, and Rachel stabs him in the throat with a dessert knife. Then she flees into the night and rain.

So far, the only resistance offered by the villagers to the Germans has been that of the parish priest who has refused to allow the church bell to be tolled. As a punishment on the district the German commandant orders it to be tolled for the Marquis' funeral, and to everyone's surprise the parish priest gives in. The reason is that he has sheltered the patriotic Jewess in the belfry. When the Germans leave, the priest drives her back to Rouen, and she returns to her brothel, from which she is finally rescued by another patriot of the same order as the priest and herself. "He first loved her for her noble deed," we are told, "then came to cherish her for herself; and he married her, and made a lady of her, a lady as good as many another."

"A rattling good yarn," as the English publishers' salesmen say, and perhaps one should leave it at that, but just as "In the Wood" and "Indiscretion" echo "A Country Excursion" this echoes "Boule de Suif" in such a way as to suggest that another obsession is at work. The peculiar thing about it is that it *has* a morality, which is expressed in that final sentence, but it is a morality that is standing on its head. The prostitutes in the story have no objection to associating with Germans who pay them well; "it is all in the day's work," they say as they drive up to the château, "no doubt to allay some secret, persistent prick of conscience." "Conscience" is a remarkable word for Maupassant to use, particularly in this context, but apparently he does mean that though there is nothing wrong in prostitution it becomes a deadly sin when practiced for the pleasure of Germans. Maupassant's morality—if you call that morality—reminds me of the funny stories North of Ireland folk tell about their sectarian groups: this one reminds me of a story of the pious North of Ireland girl, returning from a walk with her lover, who says reproachfully, "If I'd known you'd whistle on Sunday I'd never have let you do the other thing to me." But the North of Ireland man usually knows that it's funny. Maupassant doesn't.

Look, for instance, at that incredible story, "Bed No. 29," which again is merely a continuation of the theme of "Boule de Suif." In this a handsome young officer becomes the lover of a prostitute named Irma. They are separated by the war, and after it the captain, who has received a decoration for gallantry, searches everywhere for the woman he has lost. When he does find her it is in the bed of a public hospital, dying of syphilis, which she has contracted from the Germans and given back with interest. The captain is revolted, feeling that he has been made the laughing-stock of his regiment, but Irma has no regrets. She knows that she has proved herself as good a patriot as he, if not better, for though he has been decorated, she has killed more Germans. Next day she dies, apparently feeling that she is a second Joan of Arc and that someone should give her a medal.

Maupassant does not actually describe Irma's con-

duct as "noble"; he probably thought it was unnecessary. And once more, a North of Ireland anecdote
comes into my head: this time about the small boy on
his deathbed. "He called for his wee drum, gave two
or three wee taps, said 'To Hell with the Pope!' and
the Lord took him. Och, it was a *beautiful* death!" In
much the same spirit one may say that Irma's was a
beautiful death.

It seems to me that in this story one can see much
more clearly what it is that makes me uncomfortable
with "Boule de Suif" and "Mademoiselle Fifi." The
two instinctual drives, the creative and destructive,
which in most people can be clearly distinguished,
have in Maupassant blended and become perverted.
When madness finally caught up with him one of the
strands in it was his destructive hatred of Germans.

At eight o'clock that night [his valet wrote] he roused
himself and said to me suddenly, feverishly, "François, are
you ready? We're leaving; war is declared!" I replied that
we were not to leave until the next morning. "What!" he
cried, astonished at my failure to fall in with his plans.
"You're delaying, when it's urgent that we act as quickly
as possible? You know we have always agreed that we would
go together when the time came for the revenge against
Prussia. You know we must have our revenge, and we will
have it."

But this, God help us, we read very differently from
the way we read the story of Irma's death. This is
something more than the fate of a poor creature
broken down by syphilis. This is the end of the allegory, the allegory of a man who, to write the story of
the submerged sexual population of his day, lived its
life and died its death down to the last terrible days

in the lunatic asylum when the doctor recorded that *M. de Maupassant va s'animaliser*. "M. de Maupassant is reverting to the animal"—"we become what we sing."

A good many years ago I wrote the story—a true one, as it happened—of a drunken old Irish intellectual and a French prostitute who were sharing a hotel room in Paris. It had been many a day since the Irishman had enjoyed a night's sleep, so when the prostitute dozed he put on the light and began to read a selection of Maupassant's stories he had just bought. The light woke her, and to his astonishment she began to discuss the stories with real knowledge and feeling, defending Maupassant against his criticisms, of which, since he was an Irishman, he had many. "He knew us," she kept on saying. "He understood us"; and the Irishman, who lacked the sophistication to realize that Maupassant had understood him as well, argued with her. For hours those two whom life had abandoned remained awake arguing about the one writer who had not abandoned them, but had sympathized and understood, and remained one of them to the end. When I wrote the story I called it "A Story by Maupassant." I might equally well have called it "An Epitaph for Maupassant." No great writer could have wished for a better.

3. The Slave's Son

THERE IS STILL no satisfactory book on Anton Chekhov, and this is scarcely to be wondered at. He has been the victim of more enthusiastic misunderstanding than any short-story writer, praised for all the wrong reasons and imitated in ways that would have astonished him. In literature as in life he was a difficult man; diffident and evasive, hard to pin down to any positive statement except perhaps that Dreyfus was innocent or that Russian teachers were underpaid.

He must have been always difficult. Already in his youth there is a contradiction between the lighthearted young medical student who wrote stories that were sometimes less than edifying to support a family that seems to have been less than deserving. Of his brutal father no one seems to have a good word to say, and two clever brothers do not seem to have been much better. Chekhov's most positive statement about himself was made in 1889 when he was twenty-nine and had already achieved a considerable degree of self-mastery. In a characteristically impersonal way he suggested bitterly to his friend Souvorin that Souvorin should write a story about him, "a story about a young man, the son of a serf, a one time shop assistant, choir boy, schoolboy and university student, brought up to fawn on rank, kiss the hands of priests, accept without questioning other people's ideas, express his gratitude for every morsel of bread he eats, a young man who has been frequently whipped, who goes to give lessons without goloshes, engages in street fights, tortures animals, loves to go to his rich relations for dinner, behaves hypocritically towards God and man without the slightest excuse but only because he is conscious of his own worthlessness—could you write a story of how this young man squeezes the slave out of himself drop by drop, and how, on waking up one morning, he feels that the blood coursing through his veins is real blood and not the blood of a slave?"

That famous terrible letter is the work of a man of more than ordinary self-knowledge—absurdly modest, his biographers think, madly vain, Souvorin thought, and that contradiction, too, is part of the problem, for both are probably correct—and one of the most fascinating things about his work is that in it, step by step, we can see the process by which Chekhov squeezed out the slave in himself.

But, as Chekhov states them, the problem and the solution are both too obvious, and it is not remarkable that no one has really tried to work them out in terms of Chekhov's stories. Servility corrected by a proper application of manliness doesn't really throw any light on Chekhov's work. The real problem that Chekhov is working out is much more subtle than that—

it is the nature of both servility and manliness. We all think we recognize these in ourselves and others, but do we really recognize them or merely conventionalized images of them, oversimplified in the manner of a schoolboy's code of honor into "dirty sneak" and "splendid chap"?

I have been criticized by Mr. Steegmuller for falling into what he thinks the critical cliché of contrasting Chekhov and Maupassant, but what can a critic do? Aristophanes fell into the same error, one presumes, when he contrasted Aeschylus and Euripides, and Aristophanes was scarcely a fool. Up to the eighteenth century every educated Englishman contrasted Shakespeare and Jonson, every educated Frenchman Racine and Corneille. Du Côté de Chez Swann and Du Côté de Guermantes is a very old story but always new.

With Chekhov and Maupassant it is almost inescapable because for several years Chekhov was deeply influenced by Maupassant. He had discovered no submerged population of his own, so he took over Maupassant's and tried to treat it in his own way. We can see him at it in "The Chorus Girl," written when he was twenty-four. The chorus girl, lounging round half naked with her lover, Kolpakov, opens the door to Kolpakov's wife. Kolpakov hides while his wife informs the chorus girl that he has been detected in the theft of five hundred dollars from the office, presumably to buy the chorus girl's favors, and, to keep him out of jail, Mrs. Kolpakov has come to demand them back. The little chorus girl has never had anything but chocolates from him, but, embarrassed by

the grief and indignation of someone she regards as a
real lady, hands over the few trinkets she owns. When
Kolpakov emerges from hiding, it is not to kiss the
chorus girl's feet but to beat his brow in anguish at
the thought that a real "lady" like his wife had actually degraded herself to the point of begging favors
from a "fallen woman," and, with a change of heart
that turns him from a nonentity into a lout, he stalks
off while the poor little chorus girl bursts into tears
of fury and frustration.

One of the curious things about this story is that it
is almost a straight crib of Maupassant's "Boule de
Suif," though, a year before, Chekhov had been warn-
ing Maria Kisselev that Russian editors would immediately detect any pilfering of Maupassant's subjects.
"The Chemist's Wife" of 1886—two years later—could
still almost be a story of Maupassant's. Two military
officers decide to wake up the local chemist who has a
pretty wife. The husband is asleep and the wife
serves them with four pennyworth of peppermint
lozenges. Prolonging their conversation with her, they
order pharmacist's wine. Then, when the drugstore is
closed again, one of the officers decides to return and
complete his conquest. Unfortunately for him, this
time it is the chemist who wakes, and the officer has to
content himself with another four pennyworth of peppermint lozenges. "Life is like that," Chekhov seems
to say. "Sometimes it's passion and sometimes peppermint lozenges."

But even by 1886 Chekhov was writing stories in
Maupassant's manner where the contrast is more
marked than the comparison. "The Witch" has the
same theme as "The Chemist's Wife," only this time,

instead of a chemist, we get a sexton who, like his wife, is a member of one of the ecclesiastical families, and the sexton superstitiously believes that the strays who come to his house are brought there by his wife's machinations with the devil. Here, the connection with the Church gives the theme a new gravity, and in an extraordinary way the husband's wild superstitions emphasize the fury of frustrated sex in the wife.

In yet a third story of the same year, "Requiem," we have a theme that can be roughly paralleled in Maupassant. Maupassant's "Accursed Bread" tells how a prostitute called Anna insists on the marriage of her virtuous sister, Rose, taking place from her own flashy apartment. The half-witted bridegroom, on being asked to sing, sings a most inappropriate song about the "accursed bread" of prostitution and the story ends with the drunken father's taking it up and singing it as well. Chekhov's beautiful story describes an embittered puritanical father attempting to have Mass said for his dead daughter, "the prostitute, Masha," as he describes her in the particulars he offers the priest. The priest rounds on him savagely for his unchristian attitude to his dead child, but even while Mass is actually being said the stupid, pious old man continues to pray that God will remember "his departed servant, the prostitute, Masha."

Now, in Maupassant's story all our sympathy goes to the prostitute and we can only despise her brother-in-law and father, but in Chekhov's our pity is almost entirely diverted from the prostitute to her old father who is so blind in his arrogance that it never once occurs to him that it may be he and not his daughter who needs our prayers. It is the point in Chekhov at

which the passion for justice goes so deep that it affects the unjust as well as the just and at which we
begin to perceive that what is at fault is partly the
basic human incapacity to communicate. Somewhere
the tragedy ceases to be entirely one of justice and injustice, of society and its submerged population, and
becomes a tragedy of human loneliness. At once the
whole conception of the submerged population becomes enlarged and enriched.

The biographer of Chekhov could easily put his
finger on that year, his twenty-sixth, and argue that it
was then that he plumbed in himself the depths of
human misery, and that after it he was a different
man and a different sort of writer. Two terrible masterpieces suggest this—"Misery" and "The Dependents." "Misery," one of his most famous stories, deals
with an old cab driver whose son has died and who
tries to tell his rich, busy customers about his loss.
None of them can spare him the time, so late at night
he goes down to the stable and tells it to his old horse.
In "The Dependents" an old man who can no longer
support his old horse and dog brings them to the
knacker's yard, and when he sees their corpses goes
meekly up to the stand and presents his own forehead
for the blow. Never in the history of literature has
human loneliness been described with such passion as
in these two stories.

But it is not only in his perception of human loneliness as an element in the submerged population that
his work shows development. There is also a profound
moral probing into the nature of guilt itself. One can
see this by a comparison between "Misery" and
Katherine Mansfield's "The Life of Ma Parker," which

is an imitation of it. Ma Parker has lost her little grandson and is full of her grief, but when she tries to talk of it to her employer he merely says, "I hope the funeral was a—success," and then criticizes her for throwing out a teaspoonful of cocoa in a tin. There is no moral probing in Katherine Mansfield; Ma Parker's employer is a heartless brute whom every reader of the story can heartily join in detesting, but the old cabby's customers in "Misery" are people very like ourselves, busy, wrapped up in their own concerns, and if they break the old man's heart with loneliness it is as we ourselves might do it.

One of the most characteristic stories of Chekhov that I remember I read years ago and cannot trace, but it must be an early story, and, I should guess, from somewhere about this period. It is a typical Maupassant theme. One rainy night a young man goes to visit his mistress, a married woman whose husband is often away. To his horror after he has dismissed his taxi he finds the door answered by the husband. He makes some excuse and stands miserably outside in the rain, clutching the bunch of flowers he has brought. Finally, just to get in out of the rain, he presents himself at the door again, pretending to be a messenger from the florist. At this point the wife emerges from the bedroom and cries that she has been expecting him, and after he pays his visit, he walks out again past the husband, more embarrassed than ever.

For three-fourths of the story we could be reading Boccaccio or Maupassant and waiting delightedly for the device by which mistress or lover will outwit the jealous cuckold, but suddenly it is as if Chekhov threw in his hand and refused to play any longer. No, the husband is not jealous, the wife is not embarrassed; it is the lover who goes away with a flea in his ear because he is a normal decent man and he had never really looked on adultery in this particular way. Chekhov never attacks adultery—there was too much of the romantic in him for that, and he knew that adultery may demand great virtues in the way of courage and devotion—but he does not like falsehood and he does not like inconsiderateness. In this story he seems to imply that the wife is a bad woman but for a reason no moralist before him would have offered—because she is inconsiderate. The technique as I remember the story is fumbling and uncertain, but the theme itself was to be one of Chekhov's basic themes up to the end.

Gradually, under the impact of two obsessions—his obsession with the venial sin as opposed to the mortal one and his obsession with human loneliness—his whole work began to change. A new standard of goodness emerges, and with it a new submerged population of doctors, teachers, and sometimes priests. Teachers and doctors represent the two poles of Chekhov's vision of the future. Doctors can help to rid us of the nightmare of pain and suffering that nature imposes on man, and teachers can help us to rise out of the night of superstition and ignorance. In the half-barbarous society of Czarist Russia both were cruelly underpaid and shamefully exploited.

Though Chekhov's most savage indictment of Russia's treatment of its intellectuals is about a priest, it could be equally true of a doctor or teacher of the time. The year—one must note the fact—again is 1886. The story is called "A Nightmare," and it describes a public-spirited young man called Kunin who gets in touch with the local priest, intending to take the church school under his protection. The priest, a dull-witted man, almost persecutes Kunin with his visits and his passion for drinking tea, yet when Kunin visits *him* he is not offered even a cup of tea. Kunin very properly complains of him to the bishop, though by this time the perceptive reader has already realized that the priest is literally dying of starvation. Even the public-spirited Kunin realizes it at last though one knows quite well he will do nothing about it. "Father Avranny lives on three roubles a month. For a rouble the priest's wife could get herself a chemise and the doctor's wife could hire a washerwoman."

For the greater part of the time Chekhov's own sense of justice enabled him to control the anger he felt at the exploitation of doctors and teachers. In 1887 he wrote "The Antagonists," the story of a local doctor snatched from the deathbed of his only son by a husband who believes his wife is dying while, in fact, she is merely plotting to get him out of the house to elope with her lover. Clearly Chekhov sympathizes entirely with the doctor, but he cannot resist protesting against the doctor's savage hatred of the husband. "Time will pass," he says, "and Kirilov's [the doctor's] grief will pass, but the unjust attitude, unworthy of a human heart, will not pass, but will remain with the doctor till the day of his death." But in "The Grasshopper" (1892), Chekhov himself seems to me to have given way to "an unjust attitude unworthy of the human heart," and he seems to have realized it, because it is the only story of his about which he lied and bluffed like any more human author

who has been justly accused of exploiting a situation
about which common decency required him to be
silent. In the story the wife of a rather dull doctor
has a love affair with a society painter (in real life,
Chekhov's friend, Levitan); she patronizes her decent
husband before her shady artistic friends, and only
when her husband dies heroically, sucking the poison
from a child's throat, does she realize that all the time
he was a famous scientist, revered by his colleagues,
and a million times better in ordinary human terms
than the flashy fools she had spent her life trying to
impress.

Obviously, the incident had triggered off in Chekhov
an explosion beyond his own control and with it a
recrudescence of what he regarded as the slave mind
in himself—the apologies, braggadocio, and falsehood
—though we of baser stuff may be more charitable to
this than he would be. What he was trying to say—
and said so much more lucidly in "The Duel" which
he had written in the previous year—is that it does
not really matter that the doctor's wife was an adul-
teress, but that it does matter, and matter eternally,
that she was stupid and inconsiderate; and patronized,
and allowed others to patronize, a man so incomparably superior to them all. The actual message is
blurred by Chekhov's rage, because in real life great
scholars and scientists are not necessarily as dull as
he paints them, and even artists have been known to
behave themselves when a great doctor entered the
room.

But the message is clear in "The Duel" and becomes
clearer as his work matures. We are not damned for
our mortal sins, which so often require courage and

dignity, but by our venial sins, which we can more easily conceal from ourselves and commit a hundred times a day till we become as enslaved to them as we could be to alcohol and drugs. Because of them and our facile toleration of them we create a false personality for ourselves—a personality predicated on mortal sins we have refrained from committing, ignoring altogether our real personality which is created about the small, unrecognized sins of selfishness, bad temper, untruthfulness, and disloyalty. This is not morality as anyone from Jane Austen to Trollope would have recognized it.

Chekhov's later work is dominated by the theme of the false personality. Chekhov himself would seem to have been obsessed by it. In the beautiful essay he wrote on his dead friend, Gorky describes Chekhov's trick of allowing people to speak in their assumed personality for a while and then interrupting them by a question aimed at eliciting the true one. Three ladies once visited him and talked earnestly about the war between the Greeks and the Turks—a subject of which they knew nothing—until Chekhov asked a question about making fruit drops, on which they turned out to be experts. On another occasion a teacher who was visiting him began some learned rigmarole, and Chekhov, after listening a while to his ramblings, dropped a single barbed question about another teacher in the neighborhood who beat the school children. Once more, the teacher, in defense of his worried, overworked colleague, became what he really was in life—an intelligent, humane, superior man. In Chekhov's criticisms of people it was never the obvious, serious things he stressed. "A very gifted person,"

he said of a certain journalist. "His writing is always
so lofty, so humane . . . saccharine. He calls his wife a
fool in front of people." And of another, "He knows
everything. He reads a lot. He took three books of
mine and never returned them." Always, one notices,
the venial sins, the raw material of the false
personality.

The theme of the false personality is never far away
in his work. Sometimes, as in "The Letter" (1887), he
handles it with extraordinary tenderness and good
humor. The deacon, Liubimov, complains to an un-
frocked drunken priest called Father Anastasey of the
behavior of his son, Pyotr, who not only does not
observe the fast but lives in sin with a married
woman. Since the boy is beyond Liubimov's control,
the Clerical Superior, Father Fyodr Orlov, dictates an
excellent letter to be sent to the wayward son. "In
name you are a Christian," it says, "but in your real
nature a heathen, as pitiful and wretched as all other
heathens—more wretched indeed, seeing that those
heathens who know not Christ are lost from ignorance,
while you are lost in that, possessing a treasure, you
neglect it."

A very impressive letter, which delights Liubimov,
but the drunken old priest who has listened to its
dictation takes him aside and begs him not to send it.
"It will hurt his feelings, you know, deacon," he says,
but Liubimov is not to be deterred from showing off
before his son with the Clerical Superior's fine style.
However, before he puts it in an envelope, he adds a
postscript of his own: "They have sent us a new inspector. He's much friskier than the old one. He's a
great one for dancing and talking, and there's nothing

he can't do, so that all the Govorovsky girls are crazy about him." Then, entirely unaware that he has ruined the whole majestic effect of the Superior's letter, the deacon sends it off. And a very good thing he has ruined it, too, is what Chekhov implies, for what has happened is that for a moment the false personality of the deacon has dropped away and let us see the true one. Nobody has recognized the false personality but the drunken old priest whose life has become so hopeless and disorderly that he has no personality left, false or true.

In "The Duel," which so far as length goes could be regarded as a novel, Chekhov attacks this theme with superb gravity. Laevsky is a hanger-on of culture who is living with a woman he despises, and she—Nadyezhda Fyodorovna—has degraded herself by filthy love affairs with locals. Laevsky knows what she does not know: that her husband is dead and that they are at last in a position to marry. Instead, he plans to get away from her and tries to borrow the money from his friend, the doctor Samoylenko, but Samoylenko is short of money himself and he has to turn to another friend, the scientist Von Koren. Von Koren has been exasperated by the silly sneers of Laevsky and Nadyezhda about science and scientists; he knows why Samoylenko wants the money, and realizes with the clarity of hatred exactly what Laevsky proposes to do with it, so he refuses to lend the money to Samoylenko unless Samoylenko gets a guarantee from Laevsky that he will take Nadyezhda along with him. What makes Von Koren such a remarkable character is that we soon become aware that he is only another aspect of Laevsky, just as the examining magistrate in *Crime and Punishment* is only another aspect of the murderer, Raskolnikov, and that both he and Laevsky are really aspects of Chekhov himself, the artist who is also a scientist. The battle that is fought out between the two men is really a battle in the author's own soul, like that between the society painter and the doctor in "The Grasshopper."

The description of how Laevsky is finally forced to recognize his own false personality is the most remarkable bit of writing that I know of in Chekhov's work. The false personality is based entirely on petty lies, petty frauds, all venial sins, because Laevsky is a man incapable of the dignity of a single mortal sin that might solve all his difficulties since it would bring him face to face with his true personality. First he sees his salvation in one small necessary lie that will set him free for a new life, but as difficulties crowd in on him and he begins to despair he realizes that one lie will not be enough because he has been reduced to such a condition of moral slavery that each lie makes another lie inevitable.

In fact, in order to get away he would have to lie to Nadyezhda Fyodorovna, to his creditors, and to his superiors in the service; then, in order to get money in Petersburg, he would have to lie to his mother, to tell her that he had already broken with Nadyezhda Fyodorovna; and his mother would not give him more than five hundred roubles, so he had already deceived the doctor, as he would not be in a position to pay him back the money within a short time. Afterwards, when Nadyezhda Fyodorovna came to Petersburg, he would have to resort to a regular series of deceptions, little and big, in order to get free of her; and again there would be tears, boredom, a disgusting existence, remorse, and so there would be no new life. Deception and nothing more. . . . To leap over it at one bound and not to do his lying piecemeal, he would have to bring himself to stern, uncompromising action; for instance, to getting up without saying a word, putting on his hat, and at once setting off without money and without explanation. *But Laevsky felt that this was impossible for him.*

The whole point of the story is in the last cruel line that I have italicized. It is the very definition of moral slavery. In terms of Christian ethics Laevsky is incapable of committing a mortal sin, but the venial sins he commits all the time are infinitely more destructive than any mortal sin could be because he can suppress them from his conscious mind and go on believing himself to be a man of honor, a cultured man, a liberal, and a humanitarian, while in reality he is not even a decent human being. Only those who feel that they are not subject to venial sins can afford to hold him up to ridicule. Chekhov, who is examining his own conscience, does not. Through the doctor, Samoylenko, who is the key to the whole story, he recognizes that whatever baseness they may commit, Laevsky and Nadyezhda Fyodorovna are fundamentally decent people and incomparably superior to the thousands of nonentities by whom they are surrounded.

Only when Laevsky is actually threatened with death in the duel with Von Koren can he transcend himself and become something even more than a decent human being. And here, I think, Chekhov is faking the psychology, because heroic virtue is not something one expects of a man incapable of mortal sin, but Chekhov, of course, is not only discussing a conflict that existed in the outside world between a

man named Laevsky and a man named Von Koren
but a conflict in himself between the slave and the
free man, between the storyteller and the doctor—the
conflict he had described two years earlier to Souvorin.
Chekhov was both an artist and a scientist, but neither
satisfied him completely, because Von Koren, though—
like Chekhov—honest, truthful and industrious, was
more of a menace than Laevsky. He was the Communist come before his time, a man more interested in
ends than in means. He could do good works, but as
the deacon—the bumbling, good-natured representative of orthodox religion—perceived, he could do
nothing but good works, and everything he did would
be perverted from its proper goal by his own inhumanity.

It is the oldest problem in the history of the human
race, that between the First and Second Command-
ments, and it is one that Christ deliberately refused
to deal with. The deacon recognizes it when he says,
"Faith without works is dead, but works without faith
are worse still—mere waste of time and nothing more."
This is where Chekhov who, as Russian critics have
recognized, is the great writer spiritually closest to
communism, gives it up; for in his moment of illu-
mination the deacon is saying what Christ implied
when he refused to discuss whether our duty to God
or our duty to our neighbor is the more important—
that they are interdependent, and that the worship of
a God who does not require us to do good works,
and the doing of good works regardless of the God
who alone gives our good works value are equally
aspects of error.

No analysis of Chekhov's ideas, of which there are so few and the few so carefully concealed by a man who was supremely an artist, can give any idea of his total range. This was enormous, and enormous because he felt that no matter how sad life might be it was still beautiful. But to appreciate it one had to be free—free not only of the external tyrannies of brutal fathers and heartless officials but of the internal tyrannies of anger, selfishness, and cupidity. His occasional fits of savagery were reserved for characters who are so completely enslaved without and within that they never see life at all, Laevskys with no hope of salvation. The earliest and best tempered of these stories is "The Death of a Civil Servant," in which a junior official attending the theater sneezes on the bald pate of an important functionary in front of him and until he dies of despair a short time afterward tries to explain to the functionary that he meant no disrespect. Much more savage is "Rothschild's Fiddle," in which the villain is Yakov Ivanov, a coffinmaker who hates Jews, who has had a wife but never loved her, and a river by his house he had never fished in. Yakov Ivanov's coffins are categories, neat little boxes into which he tries sourly to fit races, sexes, and occupations. Categories too are all that is left to "The Man in the Box," one of three magnificent stories that Chekhov wrote in 1898, using an entirely new technique in which he merely describes a group of friends sitting around and spinning yarns from which general ideas begin to emerge. The box that Byelikov is in is one of Yakov Ivanov's coffins. He is a man who never likes to do anything unless he has found a government regulation that permits it, and so he gives up the girl he might have married and who might have saved him, all because he sees her riding a bicycle—a contingency no government regulation has envisaged. The difference between the two later stories and "The Death of a Civil Servant" is that, as he grows older, Chekhov realizes that not only do these mediocrities with their miserable venial sins impose their categories on themselves; they impose them on others as well.

He had the whole town under his thumb. Our ladies did not get up private theatricals on Saturdays for fear he should get to hear of it, and the clergy dared not eat meat or play cards in his presence. Under the influence of people like Byelikov we have got into the way of being afraid of everything in our town for the last ten or fifteen years. They are afraid to speak aloud, afraid to send letters, afraid to make acquaintances, afraid to read books, afraid to help the poor, to teach people to read and write.

As Chekhov's own end approached with a growing sense of the brevity and beauty of human life there was also a growing sense of the necessity for grasping it. It is the period of the loveliest of his comedies, *The Cherry Orchard,* and of a half-dozen stories that seem to tremble on the verge of music, so full are they of pure poetry. Here and there there is even an extraordinary sort of romanticism in reverse, romanticism as it might perhaps appear to a theologian in an inspired moment. Chekhov does not cease to emphasize the importance of the venial sin, but it is almost as though he were putting in a good word for the mortal sin, the sin that requires character and steadfastness of purpose. It is as though this saintly man, who all his life has been preaching to us to be industrious, respectful to doctors and teachers, considerate to our relatives and friends, were adding despairingly, "But if all this doesn't make you love life better, then for God's sake be bad!" In "About Love," one of the three marvelous stories of 1898, he seems to be defending the mortal sin if in fact it proves to be the only way out of an intolerable existence. One of the group of friends who are discussing general ideas—the character Chekhov's biographer, David Magarshack, identifies with Chekhov himself—describes a silent love affair with a married woman in which both, for the best reasons, are entirely circumspect in their behavior up to the very moment of parting and then realize that they have wasted their lives. The lover sums it up in his own way:

I understand that when you love you must either, in your reasonings about that love, start from what is highest, from what is more important than happiness or unhappiness, sin or virtue in their accepted meaning, or you must not reason at all.

Browning might have uttered that sentiment, or Yeats, who once said to me, "The ethical impulse always breaks the ethical law." What reveals the moralist, the prose writer as opposed to the poet, is the qualification of "what is highest"—that "which is more important than happiness or unhappiness." You may order the dinner but you must foot the bill; you may in the last resort do whatever seems right to you, but you must accept responsibility for it in this world and the next.

In precisely the same year as "About Love" Chekhov took up the theme again in what may well be the most beautiful short story in the world, "The Lady With the Dog." It is a footnote to the theme of "The Grasshopper." This story is about a young woman, married to a dull official, who meets a married man at the seaside and becomes his mistress. Like the heroine of "The Grasshopper" she is punished, but this time it seems to be because she does not leave her husband altogether. She and her lover, like Laevsky, seem to lack the capacity for committing the one mortal sin that would justify them in the eyes of God.

Then they discussed their situation for a long time, trying to think how they could get rid of the necessity for hiding, deception, living in different towns, being so long without meeting. How were they to shake off these intolerable fetters?

Easily enough, Chekhov implies, by living together and taking the consequences, though, in justice to a man who always tried to be just, one must notice that both these stories were written before he met the woman he married. How he would have felt if he had lived longer is something we can never know.

I feel sure that "The Bishop," written the year before he died, is, like Mozart's final "Requiem," a celebration of his own death. The bishop, a poor boy who has been raised to eminence in the Church, struggles through his duties, though each night he collapses in pain as Chekhov himself was collapsing. He thinks back upon his youth, and everything that recurs to him is transfigured, and yet he remains a lonely man, as lonely as the old cab driver whose son has died or the man who has had to get rid of his horse and dog. His mother has come to visit him, along with his niece, but his mother still calls him "Your Grace," putting the immense barriers of society between him and the only human contact he can hope for. I can't help wondering whether Chekhov's mother did not once upset him by addressing him as "Doctor." It is only just before he dies that the false personality *she* has built up for herself because of her distinguished son collapses, and she calls him again by the intimate names she had called him when he was still only a little boy who could not button his own trousers. It is the final affirmation of Chekhov's faith in life—lonely and sad, immeasurably sad, but beautiful beyond the power of the greatest artist to tell.

4. You and Who Else?

WHEN IT COMES to the short story I always feel a certain embarrassment in discussing the work of Rudyard Kipling beside that of storytellers like Chekhov and Maupassant, an embarrassment I find it hard to explain. If I disliked it, it would all be much easier, but I don't. I have read and reread it with genuine admiration, but at the same time I cannot help thinking that if they are real writers then Kipling is not; if, on the other hand, Kipling is a real writer there is something obviously wrong with them. I fancy it is the same sort of discomfort I should feel if I were to compare his verse with that of Keats and Shelley. Some of his poems have given me great pleasure and if I were compiling an anthology I should certainly feel that I must consider them, but once more, if what Keats and Shelley wrote is real poetry, then Kipling is not a poet at all. One could get out of that particular dilemma by invoking the distinction between poetry and verse, though it is one I have never been able to fathom myself. All I can say is that Kipling's storytelling seems to me to bear the same relationship to real storytelling that his poetry does to real poetry.

But if I cannot define I can perhaps illustrate by discussing one of his stories which is famous—and deservedly so, for it is clearly a masterpiece. I mean "The Gardener." This story describes the relationship of an aunt and nephew, Helen and Michael Turrell. Michael is the illegitimate son of Helen's dead brother and of the daughter of a retired noncommissioned officer—hardly the sort of a woman a brother of hers could be expected to marry. At the age of six he is given permission to call Helen "Mummy" at bedtime and between themselves. At ten he realizes that he is illegitimate and attempts to put a good face on it. At twelve when he has a temperature he raves about his illegitimacy until his aunt soothes him by promising that "nothing on earth or beyond could make any difference between them."

So far the story could hardly be better. Then Michael is killed at Ypres, and years later his aunt visits his grave. On her way she strikes up acquaintance with a woman called Mrs. Scarsworth who earns a little money on the side by photographing graves for relatives. Then in a splendid and most moving little scene Mrs. Scarsworth comes to Helen's bedroom and blurts it all out. It is not for the money that she photographs war graves but to visit the grave of her own lover. Already, she has visited it eight times and feels that she cannot visit it again until she acknowledges to somebody what he really was to her. Misinterpreting Helen's horror and pity, she walks out.

Next morning when Helen visits the cemetery she sees a gardener bending over one of the graves, and he asks whose grave she is looking for. "Lieutenant Michael Turrell—my nephew," she replies, and the gardener, "with infinite compassion" says, "Come with me and I will show you where your son lies."

Now, "The Gardener" is a great piece of writing, a most moving piece of writing, and I have never read it without wanting to weep, and yet there *is* something about it that makes me uncomfortable. Naturally, not being entirely unfamiliar with the devices of the storyteller, I have wondered whether this was not caused by the Celestial Gardener—the literary equivalent of a Celestial Choir—a gimmick deliberately introduced at a point when the reader is so deeply moved—or should be so deeply moved—that any comment of the author's is a breach of good taste. Undoubtedly, the story would be immensely improved by the Celestial Gentleman's removal, but I can't help thinking that He Himself is not a cause but a symptom of something false in the story and that the gimmick in a short story is no more than the consequence of all the false steps the author has already taken.

As a writer I can put up a very good case for the form of the story as Kipling wrote it. I can say that this is a story of hypocrisy that has blasted the life of an innocent child and that it is proper that the form of the story should be the external representation of all the hypocrisy up to the supreme moment when it is confronted by God and collapses. But really, I don't believe a word of it. Instead I have found myself rewriting the story as it might have been written by Chekhov or Maupassant, just to see what would happen: if instead of beginning, as Kipling does, with "Everyone in the village knew that Helen

Turrell did her duty by all her world, and by none more honorably than by her only brother's unfortunate child" I wrote, "Helen Turrell was about to have an illegitimate baby"; and, instead of the fine irony of "She most nobly took charge, although she was, at the time, under threat of lung trouble which had driven her to the South of France" I wrote, "So as to have the baby she had to pretend that she was suffering from lung trouble and had been ordered by her doctor to go to the South of France."

It does not seem to me that the theme—the essential part of the story—suffers much in the transposition, but what happens in the actual treatment is very interesting. One moves out of the world of Celestial Gardeners and Celestial Choirs in which everyone looms twelve feet tall into a real world in which people are five-feet-ten, and having an illegitimate baby is not an inspired act of motherhood but a terrifying and humiliating experience, and one realizes that in bringing the child home with her Helen Turrell shows herself a woman of heroic stature—at least six feet. In fact, the whole center of the story changes, and the mother rather than the son becomes the subject. One can see that it is not only that the son is being deprived of his mother's love but that the mother is being deprived of her son's love, which might mean more to her than hers to him. But whether the process is right or wrong artistically, the falsehood drops away, so that the reader, instead of having his brains battered in by Celestial Gardeners is persuaded into sharing a real human experience, that of having an illegitimate baby in a world in which babies can be seriously described as "illegitimate."

Now if I could say straight out what is wrong with Kipling's treatment of "The Gardener," I could put my finger on what is wrong with Kipling as a writer, but it is not enough merely to point out how somebody else could have done it better. What does emerge from the rewriting is that Kipling does not keep his eye on the object. He is not really thinking at all of that mother and son but of an audience and the effect he can create on an audience. That is to say, he is not thinking of me in my private capacity as a solitary reader, sitting at home by my own fire with my book; detached, critical, and inclined to resent any assault on my emotions as an invasion of privacy, but in my public capacity as a member of the Young Conservatives' League who can be appealed to on such general issues as "Should a Mother Tell?" As an individual reader I don't give a damn whether she tells or not. I want to know at once which mother, and what she has to tell, and to whom, and what the consequences are likely to be, and I am quite ready to be persuaded either way, according to the facts and the ability of the man who states them. In other words, if Kipling had written this story as an example of a mother's self-sacrifice it would be all the same to me.

This oratorical approach, this consciousness of the individual reader as an audience who, at whatever cost to the artistic properties, must be reduced to tears or laughter or rage is characteristic of Kipling. There is another coarser example in a well-known story of his called "Love-O'-Women." The occasion is the trial of a sergeant named Raines who has murdered the se-

ducer of his wife. Mulvaney reminisces about another
seducer and the sticky end to which he came. Mulvaney, on loan to the Black Tyrones, notices that the
man he calls Love-O'-Women is trying to get himself killed in action. Love-O'-Women is enduring
torments of conscience from the memory of the woman
whose love he has thrown away, hereinafter known
as "Diamonds an' Pearls." Mulvaney also realizes that
Love-O'-Women is suffering from the consequences of
venereal disease and has not long to live. When the
dying man is being carried into Peshawar after the
campaign, whom does he see entering a brothel but
Diamonds an' Pearls herself, and with furious strength
he hurls himself out of the cart and follows her.

"Fwhat do you do here?" asks Diamonds an' Pearls, "that
have taken away my joy in my man this five years gone—
that have broken my rest and killed my body an' damned
my soul for the sake av seein' how 'twas done. Did your
expayrience afterwards bring you acrost any woman that
give you more than I did? Wud I not ha' died for you, an'
wid you, Ellis? Ye know that, man. If iver your lyin' sowl
saw truth in uts life ye know that."

"I'm dyin', Aigypt,—dyin' " says Love-O'-Women,
remembering his expensive education, and "Die
here!" retorts Diamonds an' Pearls, offering him the
loan of her breast, which he hastens to accept, and
then, like the true Cleopatra she is, Diamonds an'
Pearls produces a gun and "dies for him an' wid him."
Thanks to a kindly doctor they are buried together in
the one grave with full benefit of clergy—Church of
England, of course.

Now, everything in this preposterous story comes
straight out of Victorian melodrama. It is not enough

to reply that there are scenes in Dickens and Hardy which are almost as embarrassing, because that is merely to emphasize what we know already—that the novel and the short story are two different art forms and that the novel can take handicaps which the short story cannot take. The novel is the more primitive of the two forms; it is closer to the children's tale in which one can prepare for a fantastic event by a single sentence—"And *whom* do you think Little Brown Bear saw when he was walking down the road?" In a novel such a scene as the final episode in Kipling's story could be prepared for through chapter after chapter until the reader was almost led to demand a scene of hysterical emotionalism, but the short story does not permit of such preparation. In fact the reader of the short story cannot be induced to expect anything. The short story represents a struggle with Time—the novelist's Time; it is an attempt to reach some point of vantage from which past and future are equally visible. The crisis of the short story *is* the short story and not as in a novel the mere logical inescapable result of what has preceded it. One might go further and say that in the story what precedes the crisis becomes a consequence of the crisis—*this* being what actually happened, *that* must necessarily be what preceded it. Chekhov was the greatest storyteller who has ever lived, but I am certain he would have reduced any intelligent small child to hysterics. When my responsibility as a parent compelled me to entertain small children, I always read them Kipling's *Jungle Book*.

In a curious way this awareness of an audience seems in Kipling's comic stories to be represented by a mania for practical joking. The practical joke requires an audience; it must not only be perpetrated but be seen to be perpetrated; and the larger the audience that rolls on the floor when the victim is trapped the more effective the joke. This, too, is characteristic of children's stories, more particularly of the school stories of Frank Richards, of which I suspect Kipling is the only begetter. It would not be fair to adduce "The Village That Voted the Earth Was Flat" as a typical Kipling story because it is miles below his standard—the standard of "Bread Upon the Waters"—but the machinery is so typical that it well repays a little attention.

A group of influential people including a newspaperman, a showman, and a Member of Parliament are wrongfully fined for dangerous driving by the crooked magnate of an English village called Huckley, and the victims devote themselves to the elaboration of a colossal jape designed to make Huckley village ridiculous all over the world. The newspaperman arranges for unfavorable publicity, the showman for a village conference which will vote that the earth is flat, and the Member of Parliament crowns the joke by inducing the whole House of Commons to sing the showman's song on Huckley.

Then, without distinction of party, fear of constituents, desire for office, or hope of emolument, the House sang at the tops and at the bottoms of their voices, swaying their stale bodies and epileptically beating with their swelled feet. They sang "The Village that voted the *Earth* was flat": first, because they wanted to, and secondly—which is the terror of that song—because they could not stop. For no consideration could they stop.

This is, of course, a description of communal hysteria, but it is also hysterical in itself—surely Kipling hardly expects us to believe that all Members of the British Parliament needed a bath and had swollen feet—but it is only a more acute form of the hysteria that is present in "Love-O'-Women" and "The Gardener." All three go well beyond the normal capacity of the individual reader, either for laughter or tears. If he is at all mature, he must at some point stop and ask himself, "What on earth is Kipling trying to do to me?"

That brings me to another weakness in these stories and perhaps a more serious one. Not only is Kipling not speaking to me in my private capacity as an individual reader, he is not speaking to me in his own private capacity as an individual author. All the other great storytellers speak to us with a lonely human voice, almost as though we were strangers and they were apologizing for their intrusion, but Kipling always speaks as though he himself were one of a gang—the Upper Fourth or the Eleventh Hussars ("The Slashers") which is opposed to another gang—council school boys, niggers, Jews, or Russkys—and expects me to belong to it as well. In fact, he flatters me by implying that, being the intelligent man I am, I couldn't possibly *not* belong to it. But I don't, and his flattering assumption that I am really one of the boys merely irritates me.

Now, Kipling had a real obsession with secret societies, and almost certainly it is connected with the hurt he experienced in childhood when his parents sent him home to England to stay with a family that persecuted him. Edmund Wilson was the first critic to point out the significance of that painful little story, "Baa, Baa, Black Sheep," in which two children, Punch and Judy, are brought home from India and left with a family of three—Uncle Harry, Auntie Rosa, and their son Harry. Judy is petted, but Auntie Rosa and Harry conspire to make little Punch's life a misery, and, after the death of Uncle Harry, he is beaten and humiliated in every possible way. He is even sent to school with Jews and Negroes, a fate which he apparently considers worse than death. He is deprived of the books which are his only escape from a brutal reality, and when he starts to go blind and knocks over objects he cannot see, the two sadists have a fresh excuse for beating him. Finally, when his mother comes back, little Punch shrinks away from her and puts up his arm to counter an expected blow. This is precisely the incident Kipling recounts in his autobiography. The story ends in Kipling's usual Celestial Choir manner with "When young lips have drunk deep of the bitter waters of Hate, Suspicion and Despair, all the Love in the World will not wholly take away that knowledge; though it may turn darkened eyes for a while to the light, and teach Faith where no Faith was."

That is hysteria, too, and it is pointless to argue about it, pointless to reply that when he says of his acquaintances at school that "some of them were unclean, some of them talked in dialect, many dropped their h's, and there were two Jews and a Negro" that things might have been worse and that if he had made friends with the Negro or the Jewish kids he might really have learned what it meant "to drink deep of the bitter waters of Hate, Suspicion and Despair"; or even suggest the obvious, that his weakness as a human being might be traced back beyond the incidents he recounts and that he may have been an exceedingly unpleasant small boy. Hysteria is not to be argued with, and a hurt child is always a hurt child.

But to understand Kipling, it is worth while to read "Baa, Baa, Black Sheep" and then read one or two of the stories in *Stalky and Co.* In terms of autobiography these continue the story of little Punch. The particular school he writes of would seem to most people atrocious and the circumstances as bad as those in "Baa, Baa, Black Sheep," but it is plain that Kipling never thought of that and was perfectly happy in the memories of his schooldays.

Why? I would suggest because at school he was not alone, and being alone was the one thing in the world he could not face. Beetle, unlike Punch, is one of a gang, the gang that includes Stalky and MacTurk. Like the newspaperman, showman, and Member of Parliament in "The Village That Voted the Earth Was Flat," they could practice elaborate practical jokes on their enemies. They could kill a stray cat and stick it under the floor of a rival dormitory; they could persecute boys who were smaller than themselves. Kipling seems to have desired no more, and he recounts it all, not only without shame but with pride and glee. Man and boy he loved to "gloat."

Obviously, this satisfied something very deep in him—something that went far deeper than the small boy's ordinary longing to be accepted. I suspect that it was an utter inability to face crises alone, and that this was something he had acquired from his upbringing as a little member of a colonial group, the impression that one was never alone or at least never should be alone. If one were left alone, nightmare succeeded.

And this seems to me Kipling's real dilemma. It was the instinct of the short-story teller that made him choose India as the scene of his best work; and it was proper that his submerged population, the British colonials—always lonely, frequently industrious, sometimes idealistic and self-sacrificing—should have their spokesman. But, in fact, they never really were a submerged population, always an ascendancy, or so at least their spokesman chose to think them, because that weakness in his own character made it impossible for him to describe people who were alone. Besides, their circumstances do not permit them to be alone, for they live in the middle of hostile alien groups that will destroy them if ever they are left alone. Their schools, regiments, classes, races, always rise up to protect them from their essential loneliness. Sometimes in Kipling a man may be left alone just long enough to permit him to commit suicide or he may be captured and tortured to imbecility by Russkys or black men, but this is always a horrible accident, and sooner or later his friends will gather round to provide a thrilling military funeral and a Burial Service according to the rites of the Church of England—anything else would be unthinkable. Punch in "Baa, Baa, Black Sheep" is abandoned, just as little Vanka in Chekhov's beautiful story is abandoned, but whereas Vanka, having written that despairing letter to his grandfather, addresses it to "Grandfather in the Village," so that we know there is no hope for him,

Punch is rescued in what his creator would call "the nick of time" by a military personage known as Inverarity Sahib, who cries in horror, "Good God, the little chap's nearly blind!" Chekhov, the doctor, can face the fact that little chaps go blind, and mad, and desperate. Kipling can't.

That sense of the group makes it almost impossible for Kipling or his readers to believe in individual loneliness, and when it does appear it is always in some monstrous disguise, such as the pit of the living dead in "The Strange Ride of Morrowbie Jukes" or the horror that kills Hummil in "At the End of the Passage." When Kipling should be moving in the direction of Chekhov he always moves in the direction of Poe. When an officer is unjustly accused of having sexual relations with the wife of a brute called Bronckhurst, the whole machinery of a secret society is put into operation to prevent the Indian servants from perjuring themselves, and when an unpleasant young man from the Lower Classes who has been sent as assistant to a bank where, in his arrogance, he makes a mess of everything, falls ill, his tough superior not only covers up for him but forges testimonials from the bank which has long ago dismissed the wretched boy, and even pays his salary out of his own pocket. Kipling is not only President of the Society for Persuading Unmarried Mothers To Tell, he is also Secretary of a thousand other groups from the Freemasons and Janeites to the Deceased Syphilitics Friendly Burial Fund and the Society for Defending Innocent Co-Respondents. Everyone is covering up, everyone is rushing to the rescue, and all the time one seems to hear the thud of the hoofs of the Eleventh Hussars ("The Slashers") coming to save the hero from a fate worse than death at the hands of niggers, Jews, and Russkys. As a weak man I like to believe that not only is God watching over me but the Eleventh Hussars are keeping an eye on me as well. As a mature one I know that Kipling is a damned liar.

Perhaps this was inevitable in a colonial society such as that of India in the nineteenth century, but it involves a contradiction which at once distinguishes Kipling from every other great writer of stories. He cannot write about the one subject a storyteller must write about—human loneliness. He has never said with Pascal, "The eternal silence of those infinite spaces terrifies me."

5. Work in Progress

JAMES JOYCE is fortunate in having escaped from the necessity of publishing either his collected or selected stories. A good book of stories like a good book of poems is a thing in itself, the summing up of a writer's experience at a given time, and it suffers from being broken up or crowded in with other books. *The Untilled Field, Winesburg, Ohio, England My England, Fishmonger's Fiddle,* and *In Our Time* should be read by themselves, as unities, and preferably in editions that resemble the originals. That is how we have to read *Dubliners,* and its uniqueness is one reason for its continuing reputation.

Joyce has escaped the fate of other storytellers because he gave up writing stories after its publication. Why did he give up? It is typical of the muddle of Joycean criticism in our time that nobody even seems to see the importance of this question, much less tries to answer it. Yet, surely, it is a fairly obvious question. Joyce was a much better storyteller than a poet, but after "Chamber Music" he did not entirely give up lyric poetry, and in fact he improved greatly on his early work. Why did he not write another story after "The Dead?" Is it because he felt that he was not a storyteller or that he believed that he had already done all that could be done with the form? It is as difficult to think of a real storyteller, like Chekhov, who had experienced the thrill of the completed masterpiece, giving up short stories forever as it is to think of Keats giving up lyric poetry. This is a question to which *Dubliners* should suggest an answer, and I am assuming that it does so.

Clearly there is a considerable formal difference between the stories at the beginning of the book and "The Dead" at the end of it, and though they are probably not printed in the strict order of their composition, they illustrate at least four and probably five stages in the development of a storyteller.

The first group of stories are what a magazine editor might legitimately describe as "sketches." The first, "The Sisters," describes two ignorant old sisters of a scholarly priest who has been deprived of his clerical functions because of some sort of nervous breakdown. The point of it still eludes me. There is no doubt about the point of "An Encounter," in which two boys mitching from school meet a sexual "queer." The third describes a small boy who goes late to a fun fair called "Araby" to bring home a present for his favorite girl, the sister of a friend, but arrives just as the fair is closing.

These seem to be all autobiographical fragments from early boyhood and any of them could easily have been included in the autobiographical novel, *A Portrait of the Artist as a Young Man*—that is, if they are

not actually fragments from the early draft of this
known as *Stephen Hero*. Apart from the very simple
Jamesian antithesis in "An Encounter" which, in a
more elaborate form, was to become one of Joyce's
favorite devices, the stories are interesting mainly for
their style. It is a style that originated with Walter
Pater but was then modeled very closely on that of
Flaubert. It is a highly pictorial style; one intended to
exclude the reader from the action and instead to
present him with a series of images of the events described, which he may accept or reject but cannot
modify to suit his own mood or environment. Understanding, indignation, or compassion, which involve
us in the action and make us see it in terms of our own
character and experience, are not called for.

One evening I went into the back drawing-room in which
the priest had died. It was a dark rainy evening and there
was no sound in the house. Through one of the broken
panes I heard the rain impinge upon the earth, the fine
incessant needles of water playing in the sodden beds. Some
distant lamp or lighted window gleamed below me.

Or take this, from the same story:

The high cold empty gloomy rooms liberated me and I
went from room to room, singing. From the front window
I saw my companions playing below in the street. Their
cries reached me weakened and indistinct and, leaning my
forehead against the cool glass, I looked over at the dark
house where she lived.

"Cool" as an adjective for glass and "dark" as an
adjective for house would have been perfectly normal
in any other writer of the time, but the two used
together like this in the one sentence indicate the

born stylist. Every word in these passages is right.
Even the lack of punctuation in "the high cold empty
gloomy rooms," a combination of adjectives that few
writers would have allowed themselves, is calculated,
and the combination itself is worked out almost experi-
mentally. Because he is so small, the first thing the
boy notices is that the rooms are high; then he per-
ceives the cold and associates it with the rooms themselves; then he realizes that they are cold because they
are empty, and finally comes the emotive adjective
"gloomy" that describes their total impression. But
because the impression is total and immediate there
is no punctuation as there is, for instance, in "a dark,
rainy evening."

You may play about as you please with alternatives
to this phrase; you will find no combination of adjectives that will produce a similar effect, nor any way of
reading the passage that will produce a different one.
This is using words as they had not been used before
in English, except by Pater—not to describe an experience, but so far as possible to duplicate it. Not even
perhaps to duplicate it so much as to replace it by a
combination of images—a rhetorician's dream, if you
like, but Joyce was a student of rhetoric. And while
the description of the experience in Dickens or Trollope would have been intended to involve the reader
in it and make him feel as author and character were
supposed to feel, the replacement of the experience
by a verbal arrangement is intended to leave him free
to feel or not, just as he chooses, so long as he recognizes that the experience itself has been fully rendered. The result is that reading a story like "Araby"
is less like one's experience of reading than one's

experience of glancing through a beautifully illustrated book.

The stories in *Dubliners* were arranged rather in
the way a poet arranges lyrics in a book, to follow a
pattern that exists in his own mind, but, as I have said,
there is also a clear chronological pattern, and in the
middle of the book is a group of stories that must have
been written after "The Sisters" and before "The
Dead." These are very harsh naturalistic stories about
Dublin middle-class life either in the form of mock-
heroic comedy or in that of antithesis. In the former
are stories like "Two Gallants," which describes with
intense gravity the comic anxiety of two wasters as to
whether one of them will be able to extract some
money from the little servant girl who is his mistress,
and "Clay," which describes an old maid who works
in a laundry and the succession of utterly minor disasters that threatens to ruin her celebration of Halloween in the home of her married nephew. In the
latter group are "Counterparts," in which a drunken
Dublin clerk who has been publicly tongue-lashed by
his employer takes it out in the flogging of his wretched
little boy who has allowed the fire to go out, and "A
Little Cloud," in which an unsuccessful poet is confronted by a successful journalist who has had sense
enough to clear out of Dublin in time. They are ugly
little stories, however you regard them, but in their
re-creation of a whole submerged population they
prove that Joyce was at the time a genuine storyteller
with a unique personal vision.

It is even more important to notice that in these
stories there is also a development of the stylistic
devices one finds in the early stories. In *A Mirror in*

the Roadway I have already analyzed the first paragraph of "Two Gallants," but it is necessary to consider it here as well.

The grey warm evening of August had descended upon
the city and a mild warm air, a memory of summer, circulated in the streets. The streets, shuttered for the repose
of Sunday, swarmed with a gaily coloured crowd. Like
illumined pearls the lamps shone from the summits of their
tall poles upon the living texture below which, changing
shape and hue unceasingly, sent up into the warm grey
evening air an unchanging, unceasing murmur.

In this beautiful paragraph we find a remarkable
development of the prose style in the earlier stories.
Not only are adjectives selected with finicking care
("tall poles"), but some of the words are being deliberately repeated, usually in a slightly different order
and sometimes in a slightly different form to avoid
giving the reader the effect of mere repetition and yet
sustain in his mind the hypnotic effect of repetition.
One of the ways in which this is done is by the repetition of a noun at the end of one sentence as the subject of the following sentence—"streets. The streets—"
but the key words are "warm," "grey," "unchanging,"
and "unceasing." The same device is used in another
paragraph of the same story, which describes a harpist
in Kildare Street.

He plucked at the wires heedlessly, glancing quickly from
time to time at the face of each new-comer and from time
to time, wearily also, at the sky. His harp, too, heedless that
her coverings had fallen about her knees, seemed weary
alike of the eyes of strangers and of her master's hands. One
hand played in the bass the melody of *Silent, O Moyle,*
while the other hand careered in the treble after each group
of notes. The notes of the air sounded deep and full.

Here, not only is Joyce insisting that we shall see the scene exactly as he saw it by his use of Flaubert's "proper word," he is insisting that we shall *feel* it as he felt it by a deliberate though carefully concealed juxtaposition of key words like "heedless," "hand," "weary," and "notes." This sort of incantatory writing is something entirely new in English prose, whether or not it is for the benefit of literature. My own impression, for what it is worth, is that in pictorial writing like the first paragraph, it is absolutely justified, but that when—as in the second paragraph—it expands to the expression of mood it is intolerably self-conscious. The personification of the harp as a woman, naked and weary of men's fumbling fingers, reminds me somewhat of the fat beginning to congeal about an otherwise excellent mutton chop. In literature certain dishes are best served cold—and these may be taken to include all material descriptions; others that have to do with passion and mood should come to us piping hot.

The most interesting of these stories are what I assume to be the final group—"Ivy Day in the Committee Room," "Grace," and "The Dead," though the last named might very properly be regarded as belonging to a different type of story again. The first two are in the mock-heroic manner, one dealing with Irish politics after Parnell, the other with Irish Catholicism. In "Ivy Day" a group of canvassers and hangers-on of a local government election are gathered in the cheerless headquarters of the Nationalist candidate, waiting to be paid, or at least hoping for a bottle of stout from the candidate's publichouse. A

Parnellite drops in and departs, and Mr. Henchy, the most talkative of the group, suggests that his devotion to Parnell is suspect and that he may even be a British spy. Then the boy arrives with the bottles of stout, the party cheers up, and when Joe Hynes, the Parnellite, returns he is greeted quite warmly—Mr. Henchy even calling him "Joe," a device that we later find, greatly magnified, in *Ulysses*. Three corks, removed by the old-fashioned method of heating the bottles, pop one after another, and Joe recites his reach-me-down lament for the dead Chief. As I have pointed out elsewhere, the three corks represent the three volleys over the hero's grave and the lament is the pinchbeck substitute for a Dead March. This is the mock-heroic at its poker-faced deadliest. In "Two Gallants" the greatest possible demand that the Irish imagination can make on a woman in love is the gift of a pound; in "Ivy Day" the greatest tribute a degenerate nation can pay to a dead leader is the popping of corks from a few bottles of stout, earned by the betrayal of everything for which that leader had stood.

As I have said, there is no difficulty in imagining the first group of stories from *Dubliners* transferred to the pages of *A Portrait of the Artist as a Young Man*. Can one imagine "Ivy Day" transferred to them? In the Christmas Day scene in that book we have the subject of "Ivy Day" but treated with almost hysterical violence; and it is as impossible to imagine transferring "Ivy Day" to that context as it is to imagine *Dubliners* with the Christmas Day scene in place of "Ivy Day in the Committee Room." Already as a storyteller Joyce has reached a parting of the ways; he has excluded certain material from his stories. In doing so, he has made a mistake that is fatal to the storyteller. He has deprived his submerged population of autonomy.

This sounds more difficult than it really is. A storyteller may make his submerged population believe and say outrageous things—that is partly what makes them a submerged population. Gorky's tramps, Chekhov's peasants, Leskov's artisans, believe things that would drive an ordinary schoolchild to hysterics, but this does not mean that they are not intellectually our equals and better. They have skill and wisdom of their own.

This is what the characters in "Grace" do not have. In this story we see the majesty of the Catholic Church as it appears when reflected in the Dublin lower middle classes. According to Joyce's brother, Stanislaus, the story is based on the theme of the *Divine Comedy*, beginning in Hell—the underground lavatory of a publichouse; ascending to Purgatory—the sickbed of a suburban home; and finally to Heaven in Gardiner Street Church. This is likely enough, because Joyce was an intensely literary man, and—in his later work at least—loved to play the well-known literary game of basing his books on underlying myths and theories so that half the reader's fun comes of spotting the allusions—a game which has the incidental advantage that the flattered reader is liable to mistake the author for a literary scholar.

When we first meet him, Mr. Kernan, the commercial traveler, has fallen down the stairs to the lavatory of a publichouse, and lies there unconscious with a portion of his tongue bitten off. The temporal power, in the person of a policeman, appears, ready to lead him to the bridewell, but he is rescued by a Mr. Power, who brings him home instead. Mr. Kernan's friends decide that for the good of his soul he must join them in a retreat, so they gather about his bedside—Mr. Cunningham, Mr. Power, Mr. M'Coy, and Mr. Fogarty. They discuss first the temporal power in the shape of the policeman who had all but arrested Mr. Kernan—a scandalous business, as they agree; and then the spiritual power in terms of all the churchmen they have known or heard of—heard of, one must admit, at some considerable distance, for the whole discussion is on the level of folklore.

Finally, the four men with their penitent friend attend Gardiner Street Church, where they hear a sermon from the eminent Jesuit, Father Purdon. Father Purdon preaches on what he admits is a difficult text— "Wherefore make unto yourselves friends out of the mammon of iniquity so that when you die they may receive you into everlasting dwellings." Father Purdon assumes it to be "a text for business men and professional men," but, whatever it may be, it is quite clear that Father Purdon knows precisely as much about it as Mr. Cunningham does about church history, which is sweet damn all.

"I often heard he [Leo XIII] was one of the most intellectual men in Europe," said Mr. Power. "I mean, apart from his being Pope."

"So he was," said Mr. Cunningham, "if not *the* most so. His motto, you know, as Pope, was *Lux upon Lux—Light upon Light.*"

"No, no," said Mr. Fogarty eagerly. "I think you're wrong there. It was *Lux in Tenebris,* I think—*Light in Darkness.*"

"O yes," said Mr. M'Coy, *"Tenebrae."*

"Allow me," said Mr. Cunningham positively, "it was *Lux*

upon Lux. And Pius IX his predecessor's motto was *Crux upon Crux*—that is *Cross upon Cross*—to show the difference between their two pontificates."

Joyce, the ecclesiastical scholar, the all-but-Jesuit, is in a position to sneer at them all. Gorky, Leskov, or Chekhov would not have sneered. Joyce's submerged population is no longer being submerged by circumstances but by Joyce's own irony.

I am sure that Stanislaus Joyce represented truthfully his brother's description of the significance of the story because it is quite clear that Mr. Kernan's fall down the lavatory stairs does represent the Fall of Man. What I am not satisfied of is that Stanislaus was given the full explanation, because it seems to me equally clear that Mr. Cunningham, Mr. M'Coy, Mr. Fogarty, and Mr. Power represent the Four Evangelists, though my mind totters at the thought of trying to find which evangelist each represents and the evangelists' attributes in their names and characters. I do not understand the elaborate antithesis of spiritual and temporal powers, or the discussion of the good and bad types in each, but it seems clear to me that this is the biblical story, told in terms of the Dublin middle classes and reduced to farce by them as the story of the Hero is reduced to farce by them in "Ivy Day in the Committee Room."

"The Dead," Joyce's last story, is entirely different from all the others. It is also immensely more complicated, and it is not always easy to see what any particular episode represents, though it is only too easy to see that it represents something. The scene is the annual dance of the Misses Morkan, old music teachers

on Usher's Island, and ostensibly it is no more than
a report of what happened at it, except at the end,
when Gabriel Conroy and his wife Gretta return to
their hotel room. There she breaks down and tells
him of a youthful and innocent love affair between
herself and a boy of seventeen in Galway, who had
caught his death of cold from standing under her
bedroom window. But this final scene is irrelevant only
in appearance, for in effect it is the real story, and
everything that has led up to it has been simply an
enormously expanded introduction, a series of themes
all of which find their climax in the hotel bedroom.

The setting of the story in a warm, vivacious lighted
house in the midst of night and snow is an image of
life itself, but every incident, almost every speech,
has a crack in it through which we perceive the presence of death all about us, as when Gabriel says that
Gretta "takes three *mortal* hours to dress herself," and
the aunts say that she must be "perished alive"—an
Irishism that ingeniously suggests both life and death.
Several times the warmth and gaiety give rise to the
idea of love and marriage, but each time it is knocked
dead by phrase or incident. At the very opening of
the story Gabriel suggests to the servant girl, Lily,
that they will soon be attending her wedding, but she
retorts savagely that "the men that is now is only all
palaver and what they can get out of you," the major
theme of the story, for all grace is with the dead: the
younger generation have not the generosity of the two
old sisters, the younger singers (Caruso, for instance!)
cannot sing as well as some long dead English tenor.
Gabriel's aunt actually sings "Arrayed for the Bridal,"

but she is only an old woman who has been dismissed from her position in the local church choir.

Gabriel himself is fired by passion for his wife, but when they return to their hotel bedroom the electric light has failed, and his passion is also extinguished when she tells him the story of her love for a dead boy. Whether it is Gabriel's quarrel with Miss Ivors, who wants him to spend his summer holiday patriotically in the West of Ireland (where his wife and the young man had met), the discussion of Cistercian monks who are supposed to sleep in their coffins, "to remind them of their last end," or the reminiscences of old singers and old relatives, everything pushes Gabriel toward that ultimate dissolution of identity in which real things disappear from about us, and we are as alone as we shall be on our deathbeds.

But it is easy enough to see from "The Dead" why Joyce gave up storytelling. One of his main passions—the elaboration of style and form—had taken control, and the short story is too tightly knit to permit expansion like this. And—what is much more important—it is quite clear from "The Dead" that he had already begun to lose sight of the submerged population that was his original subject. There are little touches of it here and there, as in the sketches of Freddy Malins and his mother—the old lady who finds everything "beautiful"—"beautiful crossing," "beautiful house," "beautiful scenery," "beautiful fish"—but Gabriel does not belong to it, nor does Gretta nor Miss Ivors. They are not characters but personalities, and Joyce would never again be able to deal with characters, people whose identity is determined by their circumstances. His own escape to Trieste, with its enlargement of his own sense of identity, had caused them to fade from his mind or—to put it more precisely—had caused them to reappear in entirely different guises. This is something that is always liable to happen to the provincial storyteller when you put him into a cosmopolitan atmosphere, and we shall see something of the same kind happening to D. H. Lawrence and A. E. Coppard, not always, as I hope my readers will understand, to our loss or theirs.

I have no doubt that if we possessed the manuscript of the short story that Joyce called "Mr. Hunter's Day" and which was written as one of the *Dubliners* group, we should see that process actually at work because it later became *Ulysses*. I assume that it was written in the manner of "Grace" and "Ivy Day in the Committee Room" as a mock-heroic description of a day in the life of a Dublin salesman like Mr. Kernan, with all its petty disasters and triumphs, and would guess that it ended exultantly with an order for twenty pounds' worth of hardware or office equipment. But Mr. Bloom in *Ulysses* is no Mr. Hunter. He is not a member of any submerged population, Irish or Jewish, whose character could be repressed by the loss of a few orders. Mr. Bloom has lost orders before this. He is a man of universal intelligence, capable of meditating quite lucidly, if irregularly, on an enormous variety of subjects. In fact, he is Ulysses, and can achieve anything his great precursor achieved. As for his wayward wife, she is not only Penelope but Earth itself, and her lover, Blazes Boylan, is the Sun, which is forever blazing and boiling—why do Joyce commentators always miss the obvious? But what have those colossi to do with Corley and his pound note and Lenehan and his poor pitiful plate of peas?

And even these, when translated into the pages of *Ulysses* and *Finnegans Wake* have suffered a sea change. They too have resigned their parts "in the casual comedy." In *Dubliners* Martin Cunningham may talk of "Lux upon Lux" and "Crux upon Crux," but who, reading of him in the Hades episode in *Ulysses,* can imagine that dignified figure committing such childish errors?

However they may delight us in their reincarnations, it is clear that they have nothing to do with the world of the short-storyteller who must make tragedy out of a plate of peas and a bottle of ginger beer or the loss of a parcel of fruitcake intended for a Halloween party. Before such spiritual grandeur as theirs, there is nothing for him to do but bow himself modestly out.

6. An Author in Search of a Subject

KATHERINE MANSFIELD is for me something unusual in the history of the short story. She was a woman of brilliance, perhaps of genius; she chose the short story as her own particular form and handled it with considerable skill, and yet for most of the time she wrote stories that I read and forget, read and forget. My experience of stories by real storytellers, even when the stories are not first-rate, is that they leave a deep impression on me. It may not be a total impression; it may not even be an accurate one, but it is usually deep and permanent. I remember it in the way in which I remember poetry. I do not remember Katherine Mansfield's stories in that way. She wrote a little group of stories about her native country, New Zealand, which are recognized as masterpieces and probably are masterpieces, but I find myself forgetting even these and rediscovering them as though they were the work of a new writer.

It may be that for me and people of my own generation her work has been obscured by her legend, as

the work of Rupert Brooke has been, and the work is
always considerably dimmer than the legend. The
story of the dedicated doomed artist, the creature of
flame married to a dull unimaginative man persists;
persists so strongly, indeed, that one has to keep on
reminding oneself that the story is largely the creation
of the dull unimaginative man himself. Most of us
who were young when the *Journal* was published took
an immediate dislike to John Middleton Murry, and
I suspect that some of the scornful obituaries that
appeared after his death were the work of men who
had taken the legend of Katherine Mansfield too
seriously. Meanwhile, Murry, a man with an inordinate
capacity for punishment, continued to publish letters
of hers that seemed to show him in a still worse light.

Obviously there was some truth in the legend since
Murry himself believed it, and since the mark left on
one's imagination by the *Journal* and letters remains;
and yet I get the impression that in the editing of the
book he was unfair to himself and far, far too fair
to his wife. There must have been another side to her
which has not yet emerged from the memoirs of the
time. Friends of Murry and hers have told me that
they seemed less interested in each other than in the
copy they supplied to each other—a likely enough
weakness in two young writers who were both in love
with literature, though one wouldn't gather it from
what either has written. Francis Carco, after his flirta-
tion with Katherine, portrayed her as a rapacious
copyhound, while in "Je ne parle pas français" she
caricatured him as a pimp. Childish, spiteful, vulgar
if you like, but something that has been carefully
edited out of the legend. One might even say that by

creating the legend Murry did his wife's reputation
more harm than good, for by failing to describe, much
less emphasize, the shoddy element in her character, he
suppressed the real miracle of her development as
an artist.

Therefore, if I emphasize what seems to me the
shoddy element it is almost by way of experiment.
Most of her work seems to me that of a clever, spoiled,
malicious woman. Though I know nothing that would
suggest she had any homosexual experiences, the assertiveness, malice, and even destructiveness in her
life and work make me wonder whether she hadn't.
It would be too much to exaggerate the significance of
her occasionally sordid love affairs, of which we
probably still have something to learn, but the idea
of "experience" by which she justified them is a
typical expedient of the woman with a homosexual
streak who envies men and attributes their imaginary
superiority to the greater freedom with which they are
supposed to be able to satisfy their sexual appetite.
It is the fallacy of Virginia Woolf's *A Room of One's
Own*, and one has only to think of Emily Dickinson
or Jane Austen rejoicing in the freedom of a traveling
salesman to realize how fallacious it is. The trouble
with "experience" in the sense in which Katherine
Mansfield sought it is that by being self-conscious it
becomes self-defeating. The eye is always looking
beyond the "experience" to the use that is to be
made of it, and in the process the experience itself
has changed its nature, and worldliness no longer
means maturity but a sort of permanent adolescence.

I crouched against him like a wild cat. Quite imper-
sonally, I admired my silver stockings bound beneath the

knee with spiked ribbons, my yellow suede shoes fringed with white fur. How vicious I looked! We made love to each other like two wild beasts.

If Katherine Mansfield really did write this after one of her amorous orgies—and in one way or another this was what she was always doing—the "copy" she was collecting was on a par with the "experience" and could only result in a permanent attitude of knowingness concealing a complete emotional immaturity. I sometimes wonder if Middleton Murry really knew what he was writing when he told so charmingly the story of their love affair—*her* suggestion that he should share her flat, *her* use of his surname when she said goodnight that compelled him to call her "Mansfield," *her* "Why don't you make me your mistress?" He was an innocent man: it is he who says somewhere in perfect innocence that Lawrence was as much in love with Frieda's husband as with Frieda herself, but surely it should have occurred to him that from the first moment Katherine Mansfield was adopting the position of the man in their relationship.

There is one quality that is missing in almost everything that Katherine Mansfield wrote—even her New Zealand stories—and that is heart. Where heart should be we usually find sentimentality, the quality that seems to go with a brassy exterior, and nowhere more than with that of an "emancipated" woman. In literature sentimentality always means falsity, for whether or not one can perceive the lie, one is always aware of being in the presence of a lie.

"Je ne parle pas français" is a good example. It is

generally accepted as a free description of Katherine Mansfield's first meeting with Francis Carco, and Carco himself admits the resemblance. It describes a sensitive, dreamy girl brought on an illicit honeymoon to Paris by a Mother's Boy who, because he does not wish to hurt Momma, abandons her there to the care of his pimp friend—drawn from Carco— though the pimp friend, finding no use for her, abandons her as well.

A touching little story, and if one could read it "straight," as I am told such stories should be read, one's sympathy would go out to the heroine, every one of whose glances and tears is lovingly observed. But how can one read it straight? The first question I ask myself is how this angelic creature ever became the mistress of anybody, let alone of such a monster of egotism as her lover. Is it that she was completely innocent? But if so, why doesn't she do what any innocent girl with money in her pocket would do on discovering that she has been abandoned in a strange city by a man she had trusted and go home on the next train? Not perhaps back to her parents but at least to some old friend? Has she no home? No friend? None of the essential questions a short story should answer is answered here, and in fact, when I read the story "straight," knowing nothing of the author's life, I merely felt it was completely unconvincing.

Knowing what I do now, I do not find it much more satisfactory. Was Murry, to whom Katherine Mansfield submitted it first, supposed to read it "straight"? "But I hope you'll see (of course you will)," she wrote to him, "that I'm not writing with a sting." Apparently he did not see. Indeed, being a very sensitive man, he may even have wondered at the insensitiveness of a woman who could send such a story for his approval.

But even more than by the element of falsity in these stories I am put off by the feeling that they were all written in exile. I do not mean by this merely that they were written by a New Zealander about Germany, England, and France, three countries any one of which would be sufficient to keep a storyteller occupied for several lifetimes. I mean that there is no real indication of a submerged population, a population which is not by its very nature in need of a coherent voice. To Katherine Mansfield as to Dickens the lower classes are merely people who say "perishall" when they mean "parasol" and "certingty" when they mean "certainty." Reading the stories all through again I experienced the same shock I experienced thirty years ago when I came on "The Life of Ma Parker" and I found myself saying, "Ah, so this is what was missing! So this is what short stories are really about!"

Like much of Katherine Mansfield's work, this story is influenced directly by Chekhov, with whom she always tended to identify herself from the time when she palmed off on Orage a flagrant imitation of Chekhov's famous story about the little baby sitter who is so tired that she smothers the crying baby. "The Life of Ma Parker" is imitated from an equally famous story, "Misery," in which an old cab driver who has lost his son tries to tell his grief to his customers and finally goes down to the stable and tells it to his old nag. Ma Parker, too, having lost her little grandson, is full of her grief, but when she tries to tell her employer about it he merely says, "I hope the funeral was a—success."

And at this point I always stop reading to think, "Now *there* is a mistake that Chekhov wouldn't have made!" and I do not need to go on to the point at which Ma Parker's employer rebukes her for throwing out a teaspoon of cocoa he had left in a tin. Chekhov knew that it is not heartlessness that breaks the heart of the lonely, and it is not Ma Parker's employer who is being coarse but Katherine Mansfield. It is not the only example in her work of a story being spoiled by her assertiveness.

At the same time the story is impressive because Ma Parker is a genuine member of a submerged population, not so much because she is old and poor, which is largely irrelevant, as because, like Chekhov's teachers and priests, she has no one else to speak for her.

It is generally agreed that the principal change in Katherine Mansfield's work occurs after the death of her brother, Chummie, in the First World War. It seems to have been her first contact with real personal grief, and her reaction was violent, even immoderate. "First, my darling, I've got things to do for both of us, and then I will come as quickly as I can," she writes in her *Journal*. What the things were she revealed when she asked herself why she did not commit suicide. "I have a duty to perform to the lovely time when we were both alive. I want to write about it, and he wanted me to. We talked it over in my little top room in London. I said: I will just put on the front page: To my brother, Leslie Heron Beauchamp. Very well: it shall be done."

Of course, it is all girlishly overdramatic in the Katherine Mansfield way, but that is no reflection on its sincerity. After all, it was done, and done splendidly.

She had always been fond of her brother, though to my mind—still speaking in the part of devil's advocate —this is scarcely sufficient to explain the violence of her grief, which sent a normally affectionate husband like Murry home from the South of France, ashamed of himself for thinking of a dead boy as a rival. Once more, I begin to wonder whether the assertive, masculine streak in her had not made her jealous of her brother. There is nothing abnormal about that: it is possible for a woman to love a brother dearly and yet be jealous of the advantages which he seems to possess; and of course, the jealousy cannot survive death, for once the superiority, real or imaginary, is removed, and the beloved brother is merely a name on a tombstone, the struggling will has no obstacles to contend with and the place of jealousy tends to be taken by guilt—by the feeling that one had grudged the brother such little advantages as he possessed, even by the fantasy that one had caused his death. All this is well within the field of ordinary human experience; it is the immoderacy of the reaction in Katherine Mansfield that puzzles me.

I feel sure that something of the sort is necessary to explain the extraordinary change that took place in her character and work—above all in her work, for here the change does not seem to be a normal development of her talent at all but a complete reversal of it. In fact, it is much more like the result of a religious crisis than of an artistic one, and, like the result of a lot of other religious crises, it leaves the critic watchful and unsatisfied. "Did he give up the drink too soon?" is a question we must all have had to ask ourselves from time to time in connection with our friends. For Katherine Mansfield, the woman, the crisis was to end in the dreary charlatanism of Fontainebleau and become the keystone of her legend, but from the point of view of Katherine Mansfield, the writer, that gesture seems immoderate, heroic, and absolutely unnecessary. No one need point out to me that this viewpoint is limited, and that it is not for a critic of literature to say what act of heroism is or is not necessary, but he must do it just the same if he is to be true to his own standards.

It seems to me that Katherine Mansfield's tragedy is, from the inside, the tragedy that Chekhov never tired of observing from the outside—the tragedy of the false personality. That clever, assertive, masculine woman was a mistake from beginning to end, and toward the close of her life she recognized it herself. Writing of herself, characteristically in the third person, she said, "She had led, ever since she can remember, a very typically false life." This is my complaint of John Murry's legend: because he loved Katherine Mansfield he gave no indication of the false personality, and so blotted the true and moving story of the brassy little shopgirl of literature who made herself into a great writer. With that sentence of hers one should compare the passage I have already quoted from Chekhov's letter to Souvorin—"Could you write a story of how this young man squeezes the slave out of himself drop by drop, and how, on waking up one morning, he feels that the blood coursing through his veins is real blood and not the blood of a slave?"

That, I fancy, is how Katherine Mansfield would have wished to be described, but Murry could not bear to see how much of the slave there was in the woman he loved.

The conflict between the false personality and the ideal one is very clear in some of the stories, and nowhere more than in the second book in which the two personalities stand side by side in "Je ne parle pas français" and "Prelude." The false personality, determined largely by the will, dominates the former story; an ideal alternative personality—*not* the true one because that never emerged fully—determined by a complete surrender of the will, dominates the latter. As a result of the conflict in her, Katherine Mansfield's reply to the activity imposed on her by her own over-developed will is an antithesis—pure contemplation.

For obvious reasons she identified this contemplativeness with that of Chekhov, the least contemplative writer who ever lived, but her misunderstanding of the great artist with whom she identified herself was a necessary part of her development.

How *perfect* the world is, with its worms and hooks and ova, how incredibly perfect. There is the sky and the sea and the shape of a lily, and there is all this other as well. The balance how perfect! (Salut, Tchehov!) I would not have the one without the other.

One can imagine the embarrassed cough with which Chekhov would have greeted that girlish effusiveness. His contemplativeness, the contemplativeness of a doctor who must resign himself to the death of a patient he has worked himself to death trying to save, was a very different affair from Katherine Mansfield's, and if, as a wise man he resigned himself, it was never because he had not suffered as a fool.

In one story, "The Garden Party," Katherine Mansfield tries to blend the two personalities, and her failure is even more interesting than the success of stories like "Prelude," where one personality is held in abeyance. Apparently, part of her assertiveness came from her resentment of the aimless life of the moneyed young lady in the provincial society of New Zealand, and during the religious crisis, part of her penance has to be the complete, uncritical acceptance of it. In the story the Sheridans' garden party is haunted by the accidental death of a carter who lives at their gate. Young Laura does not want the garden party to take place; she tries to talk her family out of it but is constantly frustrated and diverted, even by her beloved brother Laurie.

"My word, Laura! You do look stunning," said Laurie. "What an absolutely topping hat!"

Laura said faintly "Is it?" and smiled up at Laurie, and didn't tell him after all.

In the evening, at her mother's suggestion, Laura goes to the carter's cottage with a basket of leftovers from the party. It is true she has her doubts—"Would the poor woman really like that?"—but she manages to overcome them with no great difficulty. For one reader at least, the effect that Katherine Mansfield has been trying to achieve is totally destroyed. The moment she moves from her ideal world, "with its worms and hooks and ova," into a real world where the critical faculty wakes, she ruins everything by her own insensitiveness. It is exactly the same mistake that she makes in "The Life of Ma Parker." Any incidental poetry there may be in bands, marquees, pastries, and hats—and there is plenty—is dissipated in the sheer grossness of those who enjoy them. The Duc de Guermantes, determined not to hear of the death of an old friend in order not to spoil his party, at least knows what is expected of him. Nothing, one feels, can be expected of the Sheridans.

That is why in the best of the New Zealand stories there is no contact with the real world at all. In his excellent life of Katherine Mansfield, Mr. Antony Alpers quotes a brilliant passage by V. S. Pritchett, contrasting the absence of a real country from "At the Bay" with the flavor of old Russia in Chekhov's "The Steppe," but when Mr. Alpers replies that this quality is absent from Katherine Mansfield's story because it is absent from New Zealand he misses Mr. Pritchett's point entirely. The real reply to Mr. Pritchett —which he probably knows better than anybody—is that to introduce a real country into "At the Bay" would be to introduce history, and with history would come judgment, will, and criticism. The real world of these stories is not New Zealand but childhood, and they are written in a complete, hypnotic suspension of the critical faculties.

This is clearest in the episode in "Prelude" in which Pat, the Irish gardener, decapitates a duck to amuse the children and the headless body instantly makes a dash for the duck pond. It would be almost impossible for any other writer to describe this scene without horrifying us; clearly it horrified the critical and fastidious Katherine Mansfield since it haunted her through the years, but she permits the little girl, Kezia, only one small shudder.

"Watch it!" shouted Pat. He put down the body and it began to waddle—with only a long spurt of blood where the head had been; it began to pad away without a sound towards the steep bank that led to the stream. . . . That was the crowning wonder.

"Do you see that? Do you see that?" yelled Pip. He ran among the little girls tugging at their pinafores.

"It's like a little engine. It's like a funny little railway engine," squealed Isabel.

But Kezia suddenly rushed at Pat and flung her arms round his legs and butted her head as hard as she could against his knees.

"Put head back! Put head back!" she screamed.

For me this is one of the most remarkable scenes in modern literature, for though I have often accused myself of morbid fastidiousness, of a pathological dislike of what is obscene and cruel, I can read it almost as though it were the most delightful incident in a delightful day. No naturalist has ever been able to affect me like this, and I suspect that the reason is that Katherine Mansfield is not observing the scene but contemplating it. This is the Garden of Eden before shame or guilt came into the world. It is also precisely what I mean when I say that the crisis in Katherine Mansfield was religious rather than literary.

These extraordinary stories are Katherine Mansfield's masterpieces and in their own way comparable with Proust's breakthrough into the subconscious world. But one must ask oneself why they *are* masterpieces and afterward whether they represent a literary discovery that she might have developed and exploited as Proust developed and exploited his own discovery. They are masterpieces because they are an act of atonement to her brother for whatever wrong she felt

she had done him, an attempt at bringing him back to
life so that he and she might live forever in the world
she had created for them both. They set out to do
something that had never been done before and to do
it in a manner that had never been used before, a
manner that has something in common with that of
the fairy tale.

For instance, to have described the world of childhood through the mind of any of the children would
have made this the child's own particular world,
subject to time and error, and so the only observer
is an angelic one for whom the ideas of good and
evil, right and wrong, do not exist. Not only does the
narrative switch effortlessly from one character to
another, but as in a fairy tale speechless things talk
like anyone else. Florrie, the cat in "At the Bay," says,
"Thank goodness, it's getting late. Thank goodness,
the long day is over"; the infant says, "Don't like
babies? Don't like *me?*" and the bush says, "We are
dumb trees, reaching up in the night, imploring we
know not what"; while Beryl's imaginary voices, which
describe how wonderful she looked one summer at the
bay, are not more unreal—or real—than those of Linda
Burnell and her husband.

These stories are conscious, deliberate acts of magic,
as though a writer were to go into the room where
his beloved lay dead and try to repeat the miracle of
Lazarus. In this way they can be linked with the
work of other writers like Joyce and Proust, who in
their different, more worldly ways were also attempting a magical approach to literature by trying to make
the printed page not a description of something that
had happened but a substitute for what had happened,

an episode as it might appear in the eyes of God—
an act of pure creation.

Whether Katherine Mansfield could ever have exploited her own breakthrough into magic is another
matter; and here, I think, we are getting closer to the
discomfort of V. S. Pritchett before "At the Bay"
and my own before that whole group of stories because
they continue to fade from my mind, no matter how
often I reread them.

Are they really works of art that could have given
rise to other works of art and followed the law of
their own being? Or are they in fact an outward
representation of an act of deliberate martyrdom—the
self-destruction of Fontainebleau, which was intended
to destroy the false personality Katherine Mansfield
had built up for herself. If they represent the former,
then the old Katherine would have had to come back
in however purified a form. She could never have
escaped entirely into a magical version of her childhood and would have had to deal with her own
sordid love affairs, her dishonesties, her cruelties.
There are tantalizing hints of how this might have
happened, for in "The Young Girl" and "The Daughters of the Late Colonel" I seem to see a development
of her sense of humor without her coarseness.

But death came too soon, and at the end we can
only fall back on the legend that her husband created
for her and which has placed her forever among "the
inheritors of unfulfilled renown."

7. The Writer Who Rode Away

THOUGH the short story does not seem to me to be an English form, England had two great storytellers in D. H. Lawrence and A. E. Coppard, and I admire them both so much that I am not altogether certain which I prefer. In some moods I prefer Lawrence, in others, Coppard.

They are very different types of writers though both came from the English working class and, in the way of men who have grown up in a strictly hierarchical society, both were very self-conscious about it. Coppard never seems to have mastered his own feeling of inferiority and continued all his life to look hungrily at the amenities of moneyed existence, while Lawrence gives the impression that he was forever trying to assure himself that he had mastered his.

There their ways separate. Coppard was a deliberate, self-conscious artist—too deliberate at times—while Lawrence was a recklessly instinctive writer who as he grew older trusted more to his instinct and less to his judgment, and certainly trusted his instinct a great deal too much. Because of it he had one supreme gift that no other English storyteller, least of all the cautious Coppard, shares. He had a capacity for entering so completely into the natural world that his representation of it is in the literal sense of the word magical. He does not do it consciously or deliberately as Katherine Mansfield does in "Prelude," and he has nothing of the fine-grained observation with which Coppard can build up a landscape. When Coppard describes the driven sheep in a sentence such as "The sound of all the trotting feet was like a passing shower and, pressed together in a solid phalanx as they galloped, nothing else could be distinguished except the black ears of sheep dancing like dark waves on a rushing river of milk," everything is metaphor, and we know that Coppard must have kept a notebook and written down the phrase immediately he had observed the scene, but Lawrence writes effortlessly, swiftly, in a sort of shorthand, as in the first sentence of "Wintry Peacock": "There was thin, crisp snow on the ground, the sky was blue, the wind very cold, the air clear."

His attitude to nature is very like what he describes among the colliers of his native village: "Yet I've seen many a collier stand in his back garden looking down at a flower with that odd, remote sort of contemplation which shows a *real* awareness of the presence of beauty. It would not even be admiration, or joy, or delight, or any of those things which so often have a root in the possessive instinct. It would be a sort of contemplation: which shows the incipient artist." In the sense in which Lawrence uses the words,

that sentence I have quoted from Coppard could be
described as "possessive," Lawrence's own sentence as
"contemplative." Coppard wished to take the scene
home with him, docketed and filed for later use;
Lawrence to lose himself in it, so that later, when it re-
emerged in his work, it would seem to do so like a
natural occurrence.

There is no doubt which is the more effective in
dealing with nature, but of course there is another
side to the story. Coppard—in his early work at least—
looks at a landscape as though it were a person,
Lawrence looks at a person as though he or she were
part of a landscape. When in his early works he
describes Eastwood, himself as a boy, his family and
acquaintances, he blends the description of people in
fairly humble circumstances—his submerged population—with the description of nature, so that the two
exist together in a marvelous unity. Yet, even here,
the unity is of a precarious kind. In *Sons and Lovers*
his parents, the only people who really got beneath
the skin of Lawrence, are drawn with absolute certainty, the most memorable figures in English fiction:
when he moves away from them to Miriam and her
family, the picture blurs considerably, and when he
shifts to Nottingham and Clara Dawes all sense of
reality is lost.

Contemplation is all very well for a flower, but it
will not do for a man or woman, and when Lawrence
abandoned his submerged population and wrote of
literary acquaintances in London, and later still, of
Italians, Indians, and American millionaires, he wrote
of people he had never seen in relation to his own

mystical experience of nature, so that there arises in his work an actual conflict between the characters and their background. They are not at home in it, and Lawrence either jeers them for it or makes heroic efforts to induce them to feel at home. From this conflict, which of course is more in Lawrence himself than in life, springs Lawrence the prophet, with whom as a mere man of letters I have nothing to do. I am glad to know that he is supposed to have been a good prophet and brought comfort and enlightenment to many, but his novels after *The White Peacock* and *Sons and Lovers* seem to me quite unreadable. At the same time I can read the later short stories with considerable pleasure, and this points to a distinction between novel and short story which does not occur in any other writer I have studied, so I should like to explore it further.

One of the ways in which Lawrence's intuitions of nature affected his work from first to last is in the importance he attaches to instinct as opposed to the conscious mind and will, another aspect of the dichotomy he makes between "contemplation" and "possessiveness." This is his debt to Rousseau, his reassertion of the natural man. A story like "The Daughters of the Vicar" is a straightforward antithesis between two ways of life, the natural and the artificial. Of the Vicar's two daughters, one prudently marries a wealthy parson who is also something of a monster, physically as well as intellectually; the other, younger girl, Louisa, marries a miner, whose back she washes after his day's work.

This, of course, is the subject that was to haunt

Lawrence for the rest of his life, and here, as in *Lady Chatterley's Lover,* one has to recognize that it has class overtones. Coppard and Lawrence were both hurt by a hierarchical society, and Lawrence's way of getting his own back was to describe himself in bed with some well-educated young lady and subjecting her to the physical humiliation of sexual intercourse. It is a sort of ritual defilement, apparently popular among other submerged populations, such as the Negroes of the United States. But if Lawrence gets his own back on the Vicar's family he does so as a storyteller, not as a prophet: there is no undue idealization of the miner's family nor any undue caricaturing of the Vicar's, and the death of the miner's mother—one of the most moving things in Lawrence— seems to have strayed here from its proper place in *Sons and Lovers,* where, because of the author's preoccupation with Nottingham and Clara Dawes, the death of the mother is hopelessly muffed.

But there is something more peculiar than that in the story. This is the significance that Lawrence attaches to actual physical contact. What really breaks down Louisa's feeling of separateness from the miner's family is her washing of Alfred's back when his dying mother can no longer do so. "Her feeling of separateness passed away; she ceased to draw back from contact with him and his mother." It is a very simple sentence but full of significance.

The subject is really the same as in "The Horse Dealer's Daughter," where a girl who has tried to commit suicide in a stinking pond is rescued by a young doctor. He strips and dries her, and then discovers that not only is she in love with him but that he is also in love with her—a most remarkable young doctor, one would say.

But it is expressed most clearly in "The Blind Man."

> The hand of the blind man grasped the shoulder, the arm, the hand of the other man. He seemed to take him, in the soft, travelling grasp.
>
> "You seem young," he said quietly, at last.
>
> The lawyer stood almost annihilated, unable to answer.
>
> "Your head seems tender, as if you were young," Maurice repeated. "So do your hands. Touch my eyes, will you?— touch my scar."
>
> Now Bertie quivered with revulsion. Yet he was under the power of the blind man, as if hypnotised. He lifted his hand, and laid the fingers on the scar, on the scarred eyes. Maurice suddenly covered them with his own hand, pressed the fingers of the other man upon his disfigured eye-sockets, trembling in every fibre, and rocking slightly, slowly, from side to side. He remained thus for a minute or two, while Bertie stood as if in a swoon, unconscious, imprisoned.
>
> Then suddenly Maurice removed the hand of the other man from his brow, and stood holding it in his own.
>
> "Oh, my God," he said, "we shall know each other now, shan't we? We shall know each other now."

Only by isolating and studying a paragraph like this can one appreciate how extraordinary the whole story is. What Maurice is demanding from Bertie is a violation of privacy that is equivalent to rape, and rape of an unnatural kind, because only in this way can personal identity be broken down and true "knowledge" substituted for mere aquaintance. And yet the story has something in common with the others we have considered. In all of them the crisis is a moment of personal contact—one is even called "You Touched Me." On each occasion there is a feeling of acute revulsion, rather like that with which one touches the fur of a strange animal or bird, and this is followed by a breakdown of personal identity and communication on a deeper level.

Even more significantly, this contact impinges on sex at a point prior to that of sexual differentiation, so that in "The Blind Man" there is what I can only describe as a strong homosexual element. This is more apparent in the early novel, *Sons and Lovers*, where the relationship between Paul Morel and the husband of his mistress, Clara Dawes, is clearly a homosexual one, based on a common possession of Clara, and after they have made physical contact by fighting they become fast friends. But it is also evident in stories like "The Shades of Spring" and "Jimmy and the Desperate Woman." In another book I have already quoted the startling climax of the latter story in which the homosexuality is more explicit than in anything else that Lawrence wrote.

He could feel, so strongly, the presence of that other man about her, and this went to his head like neat spirits. That other man! In some subtle, inexplicable way he was actually bodily present, the husband. The woman moved in his aura. She was hopelessly married to him.

And this went to Jimmy's head like neat whiskey. Which of the two would fall before him with a greater fall—the woman, or the man, her husband?

This is the situation I have described as "the unnatural triangle," a love affair in which the husband, or someone who occupies the position of a husband, connives at his own deception for the sake of the abnormal pleasure he derives from his vicarious relations with another man, and by "relations" I do not mean psychological relations; I mean actual physical contact at a remove with another man. It appears first, so far as I know, in Dostoevski, then in Lawrence, then in Joyce's *Exiles* and has its echoes in *Ulysses*. In that book Bloom's feelings toward Blazes Boylan are, to put it mildly, ambiguous.

But what is it all about? I have never been satisfied that the word "homosexual" conveys what I really mean about Lawrence, and I feel that one must make a real distinction between him and the other writers who make use of "the unnatural triangle." In some way sex for Lawrence is associated with his mystical experience of nature; and that experience seems to derive almost entirely from physical contact and to represent a childish phase of development *before* the actual determination of sex. In this way one could explain the extraordinary brilliance with which he draws his parents, whose contact with him is something ineluctable, the relative uncertainty of his description of Miriam's family, and the feebleness of his description of the Daweses on whom he must literally impose his right to contact.

One could write a whole book on the use he makes of the word "contact" itself. It plays a great part in his later prophetic work, in which he argues with considerable force that the fastidiousness produced by modern education has alienated us from nature by making us avoid heavy physical labor and household chores such as he loved to do himself. But one might go even further and say that Lawrence's idea of the relationship between men and women never went beyond the tactile stage, the stage when physical privacy is constantly violated by one's parents and at which children caress and beat one another without discrimination. Middleton Murry once described to me how he and Gordon Campbell met Lawrence and Frieda coming down the hill from Cholesbury, Lawrence carrying his right arm in a sling and Frieda beaming. To Murry's questions Lawrence replied with a certain complacency, *"She* said I wasn't as good as Tolstoy." Lawrence was a man who could not believe in his own emotions unless they involved actual physical contact, a blow or a caress of the most intimate kind.

That is the physical contact behind a beautiful story like "Tickets Please." In this a bus conductress called Annie, who has been jilted by a bus inspector significantly known as John Thomas, organizes the other bus conductresses he has treated in the same way, to teach him a lesson. The girls, in a state of hysteria, mob him, but Annie, who is really out for blood, strikes him with the heavy buckle of a belt. When the girls mockingly ask him to choose one of their number, he chooses Annie, and there is no mockery about his choice. Annie loves him and has made him love her, as the girl in "The Horse Dealer's Daughter" makes the doctor love her. What is not made clear but is implicit in the story is that it is Annie's physical brutality that John Thomas loves. Of course he will pay her out for it sooner or later, and Annie knows it, for like him she has a profound streak of masochism in her, but she has triumphed in breaking through the physical fastidiousness that might have kept her and John Thomas apart.

In another fine story, "Samson and Delilah," a wayward husband returns after many years to the wife and daughter he had abandoned and who now run a bar in a lonely spot in Devon. The wife refuses to admit that she has ever known him, and with the aid of some soldiers, trusses him up and throws him on the roadside, but he releases himself and returns to the bar, where the door has been left open for him. He and the hero of "Tickets Please" assert their masculinity by recognizing that the violence done them is merely another aspect of the love contact, like Louisa's scrubbing of the miner's back and Bertie Reid's touching of the blind man's scar. It is an extraordinary type of psychology and one I find it almost impossible to discuss because I cannot see where the breakdown of abstraction and fastidiousness is supposed to end and where the disastrous confusion of the destructive and creative instincts that I have remarked on in Maupassant begins.

All the same, it is a very real type of psychology and not by any means confined to the working class who, in my youth at least, often took it for granted. "A man would never love you till he'd beat you," is an old woman's phrase that I remember very vividly from my childhood, though it shocked me then and shocks me now.

But what must be said about these beautiful early stories is that the physical contact in them is precisely what gives them their warmth and joy, and one might argue that the physical contact bears a strong resemblance to what we know as Christian charity. By the act of touching we accept our neighbor's dirt and smells and sores and brutality as Christ accepted them and in order that our own may be forgiven us.

But that is miracle. All these stories are miracle

stories as all Yeats's one-act plays are miracle plays, and we must add that miracles are no proper subject for treatment in extended form. By their very nature they are subjects for the writer of one-act plays or the short-story writer, never for the novelist. In the white heat of the short story we can tolerate the physically incomplete blind man who needs to have his scars felt in order to overcome his loneliness, but when one finds a whole chapter of a novel devoted to a description of a man massaging another man's stomach, as one does in Lawrence, the white heat becomes hysteria, and hysteria itself rapidly degenerates into boredom. In the novel as in the epic, "a common greyness silvers everything."

The development of a short-story writer who ceases to be a short-story writer and becomes something else is fascinating, at least to another short-story writer. Joyce, as I have said, stops dead and then resumes his work with autobiographical fantasias, written in a style that becomes more and more elaborate and in which the submerged population of the short stories becomes liberated into figures from classical mythology. Lawrence, the intuitive artist, never ceases to write stories, but their quality changes. His style, like that of most intuitive artists, had always been swift and certain, though in his haste he might often have used conjunctions to begin his sentences and exclamation points to end them. In his later work the style becomes more exasperating with its "ands," "buts," "sos," and "whereases" and hysterical with exclamation points and italics, and side by side with this his characters were changing as Joyce's changed, from the submerged population of the English Midlands to the symbolic figures of the English society papers—lords and ladies, wealthy businessmen, American millionaires and their families. *Lady Chatterley's Lover* is only Louisa's lover in "The Daughters of the Vicar" but with all the sense of actuality left out. In the form of the novel this change is intolerable—a novel, no matter how fantastic, must have some sense of actuality. In the stories and *nouvelles* the withdrawal of the sense of actuality draws them gradually closer to the condition of tales—nearer to Pushkin and Poe, farther from Chekhov and Maupassant. They are excellent tales; that sense of the miraculous which is in Lawrence's work from the beginning saves them from becoming mere exercises in the occult, but no set of standards that will apply to Chekhov and Maupassant can be applied to them.

Am I wrong in suspecting that something about the change in his work can be attributed to his English upbringing? Both in him and Coppard there is a feeling of social inadequacy which makes them a little too anxious to get away from their backgrounds and meditate too much upon the sheer beauty of an independent income. Lawrence managed to persuade his admirers that the only thing he really cared for was a sexual potency that smoothed out abstraction and fastidiousness, but this was one of the major achievements of a major yarn-spinner because he really loved rank and money more than most people and to him sex was merely a convenient method of ironing out the inequalities imposed on him by his birth. No doubt, as a serious prophet he deplored the worship of money, but anyone who reads "The Rockinghorse Winner" without wondering excitedly exactly how much the neurotic small boy will accumulate through riding his rockinghorse and visualizing the winners of the classic races before Nemesis catches up with him must be a critical St. Francis of Assisi. No doubt the child's death is a very proper punishment for his family's preoccupation with money, though why he rather than his family should be punished is something of a problem, but at the same time eighty thousand pounds—three hundred thousand dollars in the exchange of the period—is handsome compensation. My only doubt is whether the story should not have been written by Poe in his *Tales of Mystery and Imagination.*

The same is true of "A Lovely Lady," in which a domineering mother confesses to murder aloud to herself and in the open air, unaware that a drainpipe carries the story of her guilt to the ears of her niece, Cecilia, who decides to put in a spot of murder herself by talking back through the drainpipe in the accents of Henry, the first-born whom the aunt is supposed to have killed. Philosophical, no doubt, very philosophical, but really!

What is clear is that Lawrence, like Joyce, was running away from the submerged population among which he grew up, and that stories like "The Princess" and "The Woman Who Rode Away" represent his own flight from the tragic and humiliating life of Eastwood, Lawrence's Dublin. Whether either flight was necessary or advisable is something we who do not know the true circumstances cannot say.

8. A Clean Well-Lighted Place

ERNEST HEMINGWAY must have been one of the first of Joyce's disciples. Certainly, so far as I can ascertain, he was the only writer of his time to study what Joyce was attempting to do in the prose of *Dubliners* and *A Portrait of the Artist as a Young Man* and work out a method of applying it. It took me years to identify Joyce's technique and describe it with any care, and by that time I realized that it was useless for any purpose of my own. So far as I know, no critic had anticipated me, but Hemingway had not only anticipated me; he had already gone into business with it on his own account, and a handsome little business he made of it.

In dealing with *Dubliners* I have already described the peculiarities of Joyce's prose in his first book, but Joyce reserved some of its principal developments for his autobiographical novel. The passage I quoted from it in *A Mirror in the Roadway* to illustrate the technique is as good as any other for my purpose.

The soft beauty of the Latin word *touched* with an enchanting *touch* the *dark* of the evening, with a *touch* fainter and more persuading than the *touch* of music or of a *woman's* hand. The strife of their minds was quelled. The figure of *woman* as she appears in the liturgy of the church *passed* silently through the *darkness:* a white-robed figure, small and slender as a boy, and with a falling girdle. Her *voice,* frail and high as a boy's, was heard intoning from a distant choir the first words of a *woman* which pierce the gloom and clamour of the first chanting of the passion:

Et tu cum Jesu Galilaeo eras—

And all hearts were *touched* and turned to her *voice,* shining like a young star, shining clearer as the *voice* intoned the proparoxyton, and more faintly as the cadence died.

This, as I have said, seems to me a development of Flaubert's "proper word," a word proper to the object, not to the reader; and as well as imposing on the reader the exact appearance of the object in the manner of an illustrator, seeks also to impose on him the author's precise mood. By the repetition of key words and key phrases like "touch," "dark," "woman," and "pass," it slows down the whole conversational movement of prose, the casual, sinuous, evocative quality that distinguishes it from poetry and is intended to link author and reader in a common perception of the object, and replaces it by a series of verbal rituals which are intended to evoke the object as it may be supposed to be. At an extreme point it attempts to substitute the image for the reality. It is a rhetorician's dream.

But when you really know *A Portrait of the Artist as a Young Man* you recognize exactly where the beautiful opening of Hemingway's "In Another Country" came from.

In the *fall* the war was always there, but we did not go
to it any more. It was *cold* in the *fall* in Milan, and the
dark came very early. Then the electric lights came on,
and it was pleasant along the streets looking in the windows.
There was much game hanging outside the shops, and the
snow powdered in the fur of the foxes and the *wind blew*
their tails. The deer hung stiff and heavy and empty, and
small birds *blew* in the *wind,* and the *wind* turned their
feathers. It was a *cold fall* and the *wind* came down from
the mountains.

There! You have realized how cold and windy it
was that fall in Milan, haven't you? And it didn't
really hurt, did it? Even if you were not very interested to begin with, you have learned one or two very
important things that you might otherwise have ignored. Quite seriously, this is something you don't
recall from other famous passages of literature, written
by predecessors of Joyce and Hemingway, because in
neither of these passages is there what you could call
a human voice speaking, nobody resembling yourself
who is trying to persuade you to share in an experience
of his own, and whom you can imagine yourself
questioning about its nature—nothing but an old
magician sitting over his crystal ball, or a hypnotist
waving his hands gently before your eyes and mutter-
ing, "You are falling asleep; you are falling asleep;
slowly, slowly your eyes are beginning to close; your
eyelids are growing heavy; you are—falling—asleep."

Though Joyce was the most important single influence on Hemingway, and one can trace him even in
little pedantries like placing the adverb immediately
after the verb when usage requires it either to precede
the verb or to follow the object, as in "he poured

smoothly the buckwheat batter," he was not the only influence. Gertrude Stein and her experiments with language were also of some importance. Her experiments usually rather absurd ones—were intended to produce a simplification of prose technique like the simplification of forms that we find in the work of certain modern painters. Her mistake—a blatant vulgarization of Joyce's fundamental mistake—was to ignore the fact that prose is a very impure art. Any art which formally is practically indistinguishable from a memorandum issued by a government office is necessarily impure. "Prosaic" is a term of abuse, though in fact it should have a connotation as noble as "poetic."

As practiced by Hemingway, this literary method, compounded of simplification and repetition, is the opposite of that we learned in our schooldays. We were taught to consider it a fault to repeat a noun and shown how to avoid it by the use of pronouns and synonyms. This led to another fault that Fowler christened "elegant variation." The fault of Hemingway's method might be called "elegant repetition." His most elaborate use of it is in "Big Two-Hearted River."

There was no underbrush in the island of *pine trees*. The *trunks* of the *trees* went straight up or slanted toward each other. The *trunks* were straight and *brown* without *branches*. The *branches* were *high above*. Some interlocked to make a solid *shadow* on the *brown forest floor*. Around the grove of *trees* was a bare space. It was *brown* and soft underfoot as Nick walked on it. This was the over-lapping of the *pine*-needle *floor,* extending out beyond the width of the *high branches*. The *trees* had grown tall and the *branches* moved *high,* leaving in the sun this bare space they had once covered with shadow. Sharp at the edge of this extension of the *forest floor* commenced the sweet fern.

Nick slipped off his pack and lay down in the *shade*. He lay on his *back* and looked up into the *pine trees*. His neck and *back* and the small of his *back* rested as he stretched. The earth felt good against his *back*. He looked up at the sky, through the *branches,* and then shut his eyes. He opened them and looked up again. There was a wind *high* up in the *branches*. He shut his eyes again and went to sleep.

This is part of an extraordinarily complex and simple-minded literary experiment in which Hemingway sets out to duplicate in prose a fishing trip in wooded country, and it is constructed with a minute vocabulary of a few dozen words, like "water," "current," "stream," "trees," "branches," and "shadow." It is an elaboration of the device I have pointed out in *A Portrait of the Artist as a Young Man*. In some ways it anticipates Joyce's "Anna Livia Plurabelle" though in general it resembles more an experiment in Basic English. The curious thing is that I have worked with scores of young Americans—people who knew their Hemingway far better than I did—and they had never noticed the device. Perhaps this is what Hemingway and Joyce intended; perhaps I read them in the wrong way, but I do not know of any other way to read prose. And I feel quite sure that even Joyce would have thought "Big Two-Hearted River" a vulgarization of his rhetorician's dream.

However, Hemingway went one better than his master when he realized that precisely the same technique could be applied to dramatic interludes, and that the repetition of key words and phrases in these could produce a similar simplification with a similar hypnotic effect. Where Joyce writes "the other hand careered in the treble after each group of notes. The notes of the air sounded deep and full" Hemingway will write:

> "You oughtn't to ever do anything too long."
> "No, we were up there too long."
> "Too damn long," John said. "It's no good doing a thing too long."

This is a new thing in storytelling, and it is worth considering at some length. There is a fairly straightforward example in "Hills Like White Elephants," a story in which a man tries to persuade his mistress to have an abortion. There are certain key words in the dialogue like "simple" and key phrases like "I don't want you to do it if you don't want to."

> "Well," the man said, "*if you don't want to* you don't have to. I wouldn't have you *do it if you didn't want to.* But I know it's *perfectly simple.*"
> "And *you really want to?*"
> "I think it's the best thing to do. But *I don't want you to do it if you don't really want to.*"
> "And *if I do it* you'll be happy and things will be like they were and *you'll love me?*"
> "*I love you now.* You know *I love you.*"
> "I know. But *if I do it,* then it will be nice again if I say things are like white elephants, and you'll like it."
> "*I'll love it. I love it now* but I just can't think about it. You know how I get *when I worry.*"
> "*If I do it you won't ever worry?*"
> "*I won't worry about that* because it's *perfectly simple.*"
> "Then *I'll do it. Because I don't care about me.*"
> "What do you mean?"
> "*I don't care about me.*"
> "*Well, I care about you.*"

"Oh, yes. But *I don't care about me*. And *I'll do it* and then everything will be fine."

"*I don't want you to do it* if you feel that way."

The advantages and disadvantages of a style like this are about evenly divided. The principal advantage is clear. Nobody is ever likely to get the impression that he is accidentally reading a government memorandum or a shorthand report of a trial. If Goethe is right in saying that art is art because it is not nature, this is art. Even in very good stylists of the older school of storytelling there is often a marked struggle at the beginning of the story before the author can detach himself from what is not storytelling and the story becomes airborne; a paragraph or more of fumbling prose like the tuning up of an orchestra, but in Hemingway the element of stylization cuts off the very first sentence from whatever is not storytelling, so that it rings out loud and clear like music cutting across silence. Turgenev's "Living Relic" begins with the words "A French proverb runs: 'A dry fisherman and a wet hunter present a sorry sight.' Never having had any predilection for fishing . . ."—a leisurely enough opening in the manner of his period. Chekhov's "Sleepy" begins with the single word "Night," which is more urgent though perhaps a little trite. The first sentence of "In Another Country" is a perfect opening phrase, mannered enough to jolt the reader awake without making him go to see if the front door is locked: "In the fall the war was always there, but we did not go to it any more." In the same way, when Hemingway ends a story it stays ended, without giving us the feeling that perhaps we have bought a defective copy.

The obvious disadvantage is that it tends to blur
the sharp contrast that should ideally exist between
narrative and drama, the two forms of which storytelling is compounded. Ideally, the former should be
subjective and persuasive, the latter objective and
compulsive. In one the storyteller suggests to the
reader what he believes happened, in the other he
proves to him that this in fact is how it did happen.
In a good story the two aspects are nearly always kept
in balance. In a Hemingway story drama, because it
is stylized in the same way as the narrative, tends to
lose its full impact. Dialogue, the autonomous element of drama, begins to blur, and the conversation
becomes more like the conversation of alcoholics, drug
addicts, or experts in Basic English. In Joyce's "Grace,"
the author's irony gives the conversation of the men
in the sick room the same dull, claustrophobic quality, but there one can excuse it on the ground that
his aim is comic. There is no such excuse for the conversation in Hemingway's story.

Of course you may say if you please that the drama
there is implicit rather than explicit, and that it is
made sufficiently clear that the man does not love
the girl—after all he indicates it by saying "I love
you now" and "I love it now" too close together—and
that she knows it and is offering up her unborn child
for the sake of a man she feels sure will leave her,
but the dialogue by which two people communicate
or try to communicate with one another is missing.
And here, I think, we may be touching on a weakness in both Joyce and Hemingway. To the rhetorician
dialogue must so often seem unnecessary since he
knows so many ingenious ways of evading it.

Not that Hemingway often took his rhetoric to the fair as Joyce did. In fact, if we exclude "Big Two-Hearted River," which is only a caricature of a literary method, there never was much of the real experimenter in him. He was a practical writer, not a research worker, and he took from the research workers like Joyce and Gertrude Stein only what he felt he needed, in the spirit of an American efficiency expert studying the tests of a group of scientists to discover how he can knock a second or two off the time it takes to move a lever. When you compare the passage I have quoted from *A Portrait of the Artist as a Young Man* with the passage from "In Another Country," you can see that Joyce is already letting his own theory run away with him, while Hemingway uses precisely as much of it as he needs to create the effect that he himself has in mind.

In fact, from a purely technical point of view, no other writer of the twentieth century was so splendidly equipped. He could take an incident—any incident, no matter how thin or trivial—and by his skill as a writer turn it into something one read thirty years ago and can still read today with admiration and pleasure.

One can see his skill better when the material *is* skimpy and he has to rely on his ability as a writer. There is nothing in "Che Ti Dice La Patria" that could not have been observed just as well by any journalist reporting on a hasty trip through Fascist Italy—someone is rude, a young man in a shady restaurant says that the two Americans are "worth nothing," an insolent policeman holds them up for fifty lire, that is all—but no journalist could have given us the same feeling of the sinister quality of life in Italy at the time. And when Hemingway ends his description of it in a final poker-faced sentence it stays ended—"Naturally, in such a short trip we had no opportunity to see how things were with the country or the people." "Fifty Grand" is just about as dull a subject as a writer's heart could desire but the story itself can still be reread.

But the real trouble with Hemingway is that he so often has to depend upon his splendid technical equipment to cover up material that is trivial or sensational. For much of the time his stories illustrate a technique in search of a subject. In the general sense of the word Hemingway has no subject. Faulkner shows a passion for technical experiment not unlike Hemingway's, and, like Hemingway's picked up in Paris cafés over a copy of *transition,* but at once he tries to transplant it to Yoknapatawpha County. Sometimes, let us admit, it looks as inappropriate there as a Paris hat on one of the Snopes women, but at least, if we don't like the hat we can get something out of the woman it disguises. Hemingway, on the other hand, is always a displaced person; he has no place to bring his treasures to.

There are times when one feels that Hemingway, like the character in his own "A Clean Well-Lighted Place," is afraid of staying at home with a subject. In his stories one is forever coming upon that characteristic setting of the café, the station restaurant, the waiting room, or the railway carriage—clean, well-lighted, utterly anonymous places. The characters, equally anonymous, emerge suddenly from the shadows where they have been lurking, perform their little scene, and depart again into shadows. Of course, one has to realize that there is a very good technical reason for this. The short story, which is always trying to differentiate itself from the novel and avoid being bogged down in the slow, chronological sequence of events where the novel is supreme, is also seeking a point outside time from which past and future can be viewed simultaneously, and so the *wagon lit* setting of "A Canary for One" represents a point at which wife and husband are still traveling together though already apart—"we were returning to Paris to set up separate residences"—and the railway station setting of "Hills Like White Elephants" the point where the abortion that must change everything for the lovers has already been decided on though it has not yet taken place. The story looks backward and forward, backward to the days when the girl said that the hills were like white elephants and the man was pleased, and forward to a dreary future in which she will never be able to say a thing like that again.

But though this is perfectly true, it forces us to ask whether the technique is not limiting the short-story form so as to reduce it to an essentially minor art. Any realistic art is necessarily a marriage between the importance of the material and the importance of the artistic treatment, but how much of the importance of the material can possibly seep through such rigid artistic control? What has happened to the familiar element in it? If this girl, Jig, is not American, what is she? Does she have parents in England or Ireland or Australia, brothers or sisters, a job, a home to go back to, if against all the indications she

decides to have this baby? And the man? Is there
any compelling human reason why he should feel that
an abortion is necessary or is he merely destructive
by nature?

Once more, I know the formal answer to all these
questions: that Hemingway's aim is to suppress mere
information such as I require so as to concentrate
my attention on the one important thing which is
the abortion. I know that Hemingway has been influenced by the German Expressionists as well as by
Joyce and Gertrude Stein, and that he is reducing
(or enlarging) these two people into the parts they
would play in a German Expressionist tragedy—*Der
Mann* and *Die Frau*—and their problem into the
tragedy itself—*Das Fehlgebären*. But I must respect-
fully submit that I am not German, and that I have
no experience of Man, Woman, or Abortion in capital letters.

I submit that there are drawbacks to this method.
It is all too abstract. Nobody in Hemingway ever
seems to have a job or a home unless the job or the
home fits into the German scheme of capital letters.
Everybody seems to be permanently on holiday or
getting a divorce, or as *Die Frau in* "Hills Like
White Elephants" puts it, "That's all we do, isn't
it—look at things and try new drinks?" Even in the
Wisconsin stories it comes as a relief when Nick's
father keeps himself out of harm's way for an hour
or two by attending to his profession as doctor.

Even the submerged population that Hemingway
writes of is one that is associated with recreation rather
than with labor—waiters, barmen, boxers, jockeys,
bullfighters, and the like. Paco in "The Capital of the

World" is a waiter with a soul above waitering, and he dies by accident in an imitation bullfight that I find comic rather than pathetic. In the later stories the neurotic restlessness has developed out of the earlier fishing and shooting into horse racing, prize fighting, bull fighting, and big-game hunting. Even war is treated as recreation, an amusement for the leisured classes. In these stories practically no single virtue is discussed with the exception of physical courage, which from the point of view of people without an independent income is usually merely a theoretical virtue. Except in war it has little practical application, and even in war the working classes tend to regard it with a certain cynicism: the hero of the regiment is rarely a hero to the regiment.

In Hemingway the obsession with physical courage is clearly a personal problem, like Turgenev's obsession with his own futility, and it must be recognized and discounted as such if one is not to emerge from one's reading with a ludicrously distorted impression of human life. In "The Short Happy Life of Francis Macomber" Francis runs away from a lion, which is what most sensible men would do if faced by a lion, and his wife promptly cuckolds him with the English manager of their big-game hunting expedition. As we all know, good wives admire nothing in a husband except his capacity to deal with lions, so we can sympathize with the poor woman in her trouble. But next day Macomber, faced with a buffalo, suddenly becomes a man of superb courage, and his wife, recognizing that Cressida's occupation's gone and that for the future she must be a virtuous wife, blows his head off. Yet the title leaves us with the comforting assurance that the triumph is still Macomber's, for, in spite of his sticky end, he had at last learned the only way of keeping his wife out of other men's beds.

To say that the psychology of this story is childish would be to waste good words. As farce it ranks with "Ten Nights in a Bar-Room" or any other Victorian morality you can think of. Clearly, it is the working out of a personal problem that for the vast majority of men and women has no validity whatever.

It may be too early to draw any conclusions about Hemingway's work: certainly it is too early for one like myself who belongs to the generation that he influenced most deeply. In a charitable mood, I sometimes find myself thinking of the clean well-lighted place as the sort of stage on which Racine's heroes and heroines appear, free of contact with common things, and carrying on their lofty discussions of what to Racine seemed most important. The rest of the time I merely ask myself if this wonderful technique of Hemingway's is really a technique in search of a subject or a technique that is carefully avoiding a subject, and searching anxiously all the time for a clean well-lighted place where all the difficulties of human life can be comfortably ignored.

9. The Price of Freedom

THE SADDEST THING about the short story
is the eagerness with which those who write it
best try to escape from it. It is a lonely art, and they
too are lonely. They seem forever to be looking for
company, trying to get away from the submerged
population that they have brought to life for us.
Joyce simply stopped writing short stories. D. H.
Lawrence rode off in one direction; A. E. Coppard,
that other master of the English short story, in another, but they were all trying to escape.

No doubt, they all had much to escape from. I have
already remarked on the similarities between Lawrence and Coppard. Both were members of the English
working class, and—in the manner of members of the
English working class—resented it. Coppard's poverty
was of a darker sort than Lawrence's because it was
not until he was already a young man that he acquired
any education and, with it, the chance of escape that
education gives. He loved Oxford as Newman and
Arnold loved it, but he went there as a clerk, not

as a student. Yeats's description of Keats—"his face and nose pressed to a sweetshop window"—harsh as it is, describes Coppard for me. Apprenticed at the age of nine to a Whitechapel tailor, he had a cruel childhood, and described it in a group of stories in which he calls himself "Johnny Flynn"—the name by which in later life he was known to his family and friends. In these stories there is a terrible note of anguish and self-pity, as in the child's prayer: "O God, make him give me a penny tonight, only a penny; make him give me a penny, please God. Amen." The prayer was not answered, and I suspect that Flynn never forgave God or the English upper classes for it.

The child's prayer for the penny later becomes the prayer of the grown writer in "Luxury" for personal security and personal freedom.

The garden is all right, and literature is all right, only I live too much on porridge. It isn't the privation itself, it's the things privation makes a man do. It makes a man do things he ought not want to do, it makes him mean, It makes him *feel* mean, I tell you, and if he feels mean and thinks mean he writes meanly, that's how it is.

It isn't how it is, and I don't think it ever made Coppard write meanly, though once, enraged by a poor book of his, I called his preoccupation with money "an unearned income complex." All the same, I don't think one can understand his work without keeping it in mind.

The other thing—the preoccupation with personal freedom—he shared with many of his generation, who have been denigrated and partly rehabilitated as "Georgians." Coppard was a Georgian in the same

way that Robert Frost, Edward Thomas, Edmund
Blunden, and a score of others were Georgians, and
he shared their obsession with personal freedom—
freedom from responsibilities, freedom from conventions—particularly sexual conventions; freedom from
duties to state and church, above all, freedom from
the tyranny of money. It was a healthy and necessary
reaction, as the almost inordinate sense of responsibility in the work of C. P. Snow in our own time is
a healthy and necessary reaction.

And in those days a very little money was enough
to set a writer free for serious work. There were still
plenty of reviews that would pay a guinea for a critical article, and a single man could live for quite
a while on a guinea. In spite of their latter-day admirers, the young writers were not violently attracted
by rabbits and pheasants, but there were always un-
tenanted mills or barges on the Thames, and one
could rent a beautiful Elizabethan cottage (without
water or light) for a few pounds a year, and in those
English villages that had been dead for two generations one had the most beautiful background in the
world and a personal freedom that was an adequate
substitute for life in the Latin Quarter. Coppard
rented a cottage, lived in a caravan, and set off on
walking tours through Europe. He was a fine stylist
and could have made a fortune as a writer of popular
travel books: "Mr. Lightfoot in the Green Isle" and
"Rummy" can always make an Irishman homesick,
and few writers did Italy so proud.

Full and bright the moon, but it did not seem to light
up the gulf; the water had no sparkle, there was only a
gloomy movement of purple bulk. All the eastern heaven

in the direction of Leghorn was menaced by a cloud as
high and wide as ten thousand mountains, and every few
minutes it was ripped by lightning that made no sound.
But the white villas by the sea glimmered carelessly in the
moonlight; the fine trees, the olives, the palms, were still,
and you knew of the water only by the white foam squan-
dering round the rocks. At one station perched on a ledge
of mountain Beamish could see down into a courtyard
below him; there was a clothes line stretched across the
yard, and on the line a pair of trousers inside out—how
white the pockets were!—was hanging to dry. Immense and
clear on the wall of a palazzo near by, the shadow of an
ancient empty lantern hoisted above a gateway was thrown
by a neighbouring street lamp. It was half past nine, though
the clock tower showed but a quarter to four, and the town
seemed empty, lifeless, soundless, stone quiet, until the
train moved again. Then the trousers on the line began
to toss violently in a sudden thrust of wind, and the lantern
shadow on the wall was waving to and fro.

In the early books of stories, particularly *The Black
Dog* (1923) and the magnificent *Fishmonger's Fiddle*
(1925), the sense of personal freedom creates the feeling of a country being looked at again in an entirely
new way. It even creates the feeling of the form itself
being handled in a new way. Most storytellers see
the short story first as a convention that appeals to
them: the convention of Chekhov, the convention of
Maupassant—in America nowadays, the convention
of Joyce—and it is only as their work develops that
they create a convention of their own. Coppard knew
Chekhov and Maupassant backward, but he never
settles for one convention rather than the other, or
indeed for any convention other than his own need
to grip the reader by the lapel and make him listen.
As a result, his formal range is remarkable—greater

I should say than that of any other storyteller. A story like "The Field of Mustard" might be an exercise in the manner of Chekhov; others suggest Maupassant; others still seem to be folk tales like those of Hardy: "At Laban's Well" could be a prose version of a poem by Robert Frost, while "Mr. Lightfoot in the Green Isle" is merely a skittish description of a walking tour in Ireland which might have appeared in a travel magazine. In the publisher's advertisement for *The Dark-Eyed Lady* (1947), there is a passage that, for all its unendurable archness, must have been written by Coppard himself, since it defines so clearly his attitude to the art of storytelling. "His tales have appeared in all sorts of journals and magazines, from those designed for the lofty, beetling brow to those for the ignoble noddle—all's one to this writer." It is ironic that the author of such stories should never have become popular, but this sentence, like all truthful statements of a writer's aims, defines not only Coppard's range but his limitations.

One can trace his feeling of freedom even better in his tendency to prefer quality—in the painter's sense of the word—to design. What this meant in practice to Coppard was that whenever a character entered a restaurant or a railway carriage there should be someone or something there for him to observe, even when this distracted from the character's own preoccupation. He might have just visited the hospital where his sweetheart was dying or the prison where his only son was awaiting execution, but having a bit of Coppard in him, he could never resist a momentary interest in an old gentleman with a passion for Hittite. This is perfectly true and within the experi-

ence of everybody. Some nervous weakness drives us
to cheerful irrelevancies even when we are anticipat-
ing what we know perfectly well will be the end of
the world for us.

Technically what it means is that to write a story
resembling the best of Coppard we should have to
carry a notebook and jot down the details of every
moment of interest and pleasure—the appearance of
a house of landscape, the effects of lighting, the impression of characters glimpsed in passing, with their
actual words. Then we should have to work these notes
into the texture of whatever story we happened to be
writing until every paragraph tended to be a complete
work of art, like the paragraph I have quoted from
"The Wildgoose Chase."

Like Whitman, watching the live oak in Louisiana,
"I know I could not do it," but that, I suspect, is how
the great early Coppard stories were written. In these
the surface of the story is always exquisitely rendered
—the glimpses of landscape, the snatches of conversation overheard, the odd names of villages and people,
the illiterate shop signs—even the comments in the
visitors' book in country inns. I am sure that Coppard
actually noted something like the entry in the visitors'
book that "recorded the immense gratification of the
Dredging Department of the London and So-and-So
Railway" and the gratitude of the Plaistow policemen
—"To satisfy thirty-one policemen is no mean fete. We
are confident there is no more comfortable hostile
place to put up than at Tumble Down Dick's." I feel
sure he had seen something like the parson's sign that
read "Moore the Marryer—Christenings Done Here"
and the ironmonger's that read "Kitchen Late Kettle,"

for, in Hardy's lovely words, "He was a man who used to notice such things." It is even revealed to me that I remember an Irish village where the butcher named Kidney advertises himself as "Kidney for Meat," a detail that would have made Coppard happy for a week and that would inevitably have appeared in a story.

The landscape, too, seen in sudden vivid flashes like jottings from a painter's notebook is surely the moment caught and held in a brilliant sentence or two. "Oppidan was startled by a flock of starlings that slid across the evening with the steady movement of a cloud." Or the picture of sheep being driven to the pool:

The sound of all the trotting feet was like a passing shower and, pressed together in a solid phalanx as they galloped, nothing else could be distinguished except the black ears of sheep dancing like dark waves on a rushing river of milk.

But though Coppard may have thought that he wrote for every sort of magazine and in every sort of manner, there was one kind of story that he wrote again and again as though he were in the grip of some inner compulsion. That is the story in which the motivation is given by some woman's secretiveness. Clearly, some personal experience was responsible for the way Coppard came back to the subject again and again, and even, in his later, more garrulous stories, recovered much of his mastery when he handled it afresh.

The early *Adam and Eve and Pinch Me* (1921) contains "Dusky Ruth," one of his most beautiful and characteristic stories. It describes a walker—as it might

be Coppard himself—who comes to an inn in the
Cotswolds where he meets an attractive barmaid. After
some dalliance she agrees to come to his room that
night, but when she does so she bursts into tears,
and, instead of making love to her, the walker spends
his time comforting her for some secret grief he never
understands. Next morning as he leaves the inn she
gives him a radiant smile, and the meaning of this,
too, eludes him.

If Somerset Maugham had told that story, the
woman's smile would have left us in no doubt of his
meaning, the meaning of the old song:

> He that will not when he may
> He shall not when he wold.

But this, of course, is not Coppard's meaning at
all. He was fascinated primarily by women's secretiveness: it is the theme of most of his great stories, and
I fancy one could almost trace his decline as a writer
by confining oneself to the stories in which it recurs.
In *Fishmonger's Fiddle* (1925), which is probably
Coppard's finest book, it occurs in several forms. "The
Watercress Girl"—a wonderful story comparable with
the best of Chekhov's—describes how Mary Mc-
Dowall has a love affair with Frank Oppidan and
gradually finds him cooling. A baby is born to her
and dies, unknown to Frank, who is planning to
marry a girl called Elizabeth with a little money. "To
Mary's mind that presented itself as a treachery to
their child, the tiny body buried under a beehive in
the garden. That Frank was unaware made no difference to the girl's fierce mood; it was treachery." Once

more, the passion exists only because Mary has kept the child's birth a secret from Frank, and because of that she can throw vitriol at Elizabeth and destroy her looks for ever.

Her words when she is sentenced are the perfection of "quality" in Coppard's work—the few broken phrases that serve to distinguish Mary from every other passionate woman in the world. Here we are far from Flaubert, Maupassant, and the cab horse. Even the punctuation seems deliberate, as though Coppard had invented it to describe the heavy breathing of a hunted woman in an English country court-house. " 'Twas he made me a parent, but he was never a man himself. He took advantage; it was mean, I love Christianity." If that did not come straight out of Coppard's collection of press cuttings it should have; it has an air of absolute authenticity.

The ending of the story is equally authentic. On Mary's release from jail Frank arrives, intending to "mark" her as she has marked Elizabeth, but the revelation that he has been a father changes him as it changes Mary. Her secret is no longer her own and hatred for Frank drops away.

The theme of "The Higgler," a more famous story, is the same. The girl in this, who has a little fortune of her own, loves the Higgler, but is too shy and secretive to hint at it to him, so she forces her mother, who disapproves of him, to act as matchmaker. The Higgler, knowing the old lady's business head, con-cludes that her daughter is a bad bargain and marries instead a stupid girl without a penny. In both stories we catch a glimpse of Coppard's preoccupation with money, but a glimpse only, for it is kept in its proper place as part of the necessary condition of life.

But in "The Little Mistress"—an enchanting story —money, which has been a mere incidental in the other stories, intrudes, and with it an excess of what I have already described as "quality." It describes how a flighty woman with a devoted and long-suffering husband discovers that her ugly maid is reading the letters she receives from her lover and gradually grows to despise him and her own infidelity, which—if I understand the story correctly—is attractive to her mainly because of the mystery with which she surrounds it. But Francesca isn't only well-to-do; she seems to share Coppard's delight in the irrelevant and unexpected until even a careful reader begins to forget the number he started with. While she and Goneril, the flighty and the virtuous girl, discuss the meaning of life, a horse is being shod in the stable nearby, and the smith and carter discuss the meaning of horses at inordinate length.

"What was that you was a-going to say, Archie?"

"To say, Ted?" the carter questioned, "to say? What *was* I a-going to say?"

"Ah, I can't tell you, Archie. Only God Almighty could do that, but it were summat about this 'ere hoss, I believe."

At this point the reader is strongly tempted to ask what it was that Coppard was a-going to say.

But the typical Coppard situation is that of "A Wildgoose Chase," from which I have already quoted the beautiful description of the Italian Riviera. In this story, Martin Beamish, a man with an inherited income of "six or seven hundred a year" (notice the casual way in which the figure is thrown off) decides to separate from his wife for a period "without restrictions." This has apparently been a dream of Beamish's for many years, as it has, perhaps been that of other husbands, but Beamish is fortunate in having the "six or seven hundred a year" that it takes. The experiment does not work out too well. "Exulting in his escape—how simple it was!—and retrieving so whatever it was he had wanted to retrieve, he made only a modest use of the occasion because he had no clear idea of what he wanted to be at except to be going, going, going . . ." so he ends up at the British Museum, reading archaeology. By the time he tires of it his wife has gone to the Riviera where she is apparently studying something other than archaeology. This is too much for him and he follows her. After a few days she agrees to come back with him and he nobly decides to ignore the issue of the other man, if any. But by the time they reach Dijon he has revealed that he thinks she merely invented the other man to bring him to heel, and his wife leaves him for good and all.

It is a beautiful story and true of most of us. Athalie's "mystery" is the essence of her beauty. Lost, she becomes alluring again, rediscovered she becomes a bore, but when her mystery is violated and she flees, she becomes again all the beauty in the world.

All the beauty in the world—and for a miserable six or seven hundred a year!

In *The Field of Mustard* (1926) the money problem seems to get even more out of hand. The title story —one of Coppard's masterpieces—describes two poor

country women, both of whom have had love affairs
with a frolicsome gamekeeper: years later, when both
are broken by life, they reveal the truth to each other,
but the revelation no longer means anything to them.
"O God," sighs one in words that have the poignancy
of Mary McDowall's cry from the dock, "cradle and
grave is all there is for we." But "Olive and Camilla"
handles the theme in a much less satisfactory way.
These two girls have lived together for years, apparently quite content with each other's company,
until Olive takes to drink and the gardener, and the
fact emerges that all through their relationship
the men Olive had thought of as suitors were really
Camilla's lovers. Like the Beamishes of "A Wildgoose
Chase" the two girls are in comfortable circumstances
for if, at the beginning of the story "Olive had enough
money to do as she modestly liked" while Camilla
"had nothing except a grandmother," the grandmother
obligingly dies of dropsy "and left her a fortune." I
am afraid I heave a deep sigh over that "fortune";
it is even worse than Beamish's "six or seven hundred
a year" and worlds removed from the little bit of
money that attracts the Higgler and Frank Oppidan.
"His face and nose pressed to a sweetshop window"
is a line that comes more strongly to mind. The
reader may even forgive my rude description of it as
"an unearned income complex."

The treatment is even more casual. It is a fine story,
but I have to put my finger on passage after passage
in which Coppard's mania for quality has run away
with him and played hell with the design. I know
that in earlier stories he has made fun of it, but the
digressions were sufficiently amusing to justify the

joke. In "Olive and Camilla" the joke has gone too far. It begins with a discussion of suicide and we are told the story of the "cook in Leamington who swallowed ground glass in her porridge, pounds and pounds, and nothing came of it," and then it continues with the scene in the railway carriage when a soda water bottle bursts and drenches Olive. She has to change and, of course, leaves her corsets behind—a shameless digression developed with shameless inconsequence.

Camilla firmly declared that the young Frenchwoman who had travelled with them in the morning must have stolen them.

"What for?" asked Olive.

"Well, what do people steal things for?" There was an air of pellucid reason in Camilla's question, but Olive was scornful.

"Corsets!" she exclaimed.

"I knew a cripple once," declared Olive, "who stole an ear trumpet."

No doubt one of these days a graduate student will prepare a dissertation on Coppard which will show that the loss of Olive's corsets is symbolic of her forthcoming loss of virtue and he will have no difficulty in explaining the cook's swallowing of ground glass and the cripple's theft of the ear trumpet, but all the same I find myself reaching out for a very soft black pencil. It is not, God knows, that I want to eliminate the thing that delights me in Coppard, the accidental and incidental, the queer people in the dining room when the hero walks in, the noises and the feeling of a real and beautiful world outside in which the parson describes himself as "Moore the

Marryer" and the ironmonger's shop is that of
"Kitchen Late Kettle." It is because all the characters
are being taken out and replaced by Coppard himself;
because the wonderful sense of personal freedom that
for a time penetrated and leavened the dull mass of
Necessity has begun to get out of hand and the necessary daily bread has started to blow up into a thin
feathery pastry. To be quite so much at ease with the
logic of circumstance—the power of things, which
the Spanish poet tells us can do more than Hercules
himself—is to be a thoroughgoing romantic, and, what
is more, a romantic with an independent income.
Olive and Camilla are delightful girls, but I wish
someone would attach a few weights to them: they do
so badly need a job in an office to keep them quiet
between nine and five.

Nine and five for unmarried women, seven and
twelve—with time off—for the others, the hours they
must offer to Necessity are those one wants to fill in
in so many fine Coppard stories. Take "Emergency
Exit" (1935). It is the tale of a rich girl (naturally),
who, finding herself pregnant by an Italian gentleman who doesn't attract her (of course), emigrates to
Canada (where better?), and sets up house with a
military officer named McNair whom she does not
marry (why should she?). "We did intend to, really,
at some time," she says, "but we kept putting it off
and putting it off until in the end it did not seem
worth while; and a year or two ago we separated,
finally" (just like that!). Elizabeth returns to England
with her ten-year-old son and stays in the home of
her mother and aunt who believe her to be married
to McNair, and falls in love with a painter called

Vicary Vines who lives in a cottage not unlike the cottage the liberated Coppard might have lived in. Before Elizabeth can marry Vicary she must, so to speak, kill off the husband who is not a husband, but in the end, her son so dislikes the thought of her re-marriage that we are left with the impression that she probably returns to the supposedly dead McNair, who has come to England to look her up.

It is obvious that Coppard is deeply attracted by the woman and admires the perfect freedom of her behavior, even to her irritation when Vicary Vines shows himself shy of entering her bedroom, but it never seems to have occurred to him that from the point of view of the suspicious reader what he seems to be admiring is a very large income indeed, or that the reader might ask himself exactly how Elizabeth would have behaved if her income had been say, half what it was; or even how she would have behaved if only she had the responsibility of earning her own living, or—as an extreme hypothesis—how she would have behaved if she had to support an invalid father. Freedom and necessity—those two poles between which we mortals must live—are getting far too close to the old poles of wealth and poverty we know from Victorian romances. That there is a relationship between them no sensible man would deny; that they are identical is an idea that experience rejects. One begins to do sums, equating conduct with cash, and arrives at such conclusions as that for five hundred pounds one can afford an illegitimate child, for one thousand pounds a lover on the Riviera, for fifteen hundred pounds bigamy, and for a clear two thousand bigamy and a love affair with an American Indian.

God what a little accident of gold
Fences our weakness from the wolves of old!

Scawen Blunt was right, but at least the wolves in
his poem are real wolves, not expensive life-sized
specimens from a toyshop menagerie. For all his
wealth and all his love affairs, Blunt got himself into
a real Irish jail.

This is one of the problems of literature in the
period after the First World War, and it is a particular problem with Coppard, though it becomes clear
only when he is no longer capable of breathing all his
genius into it. And it is at this point that I begin
to wonder whether Coppard's favorite subject is not
one best suited to comedy, or even farce; whether, in
fact, the particular sort of freedom he longs for is
really personal freedom at all and not merely a new
form of the old naturalistic compulsion that put a
man's nose to the grindstone and never admitted the
possibility of his raising it again. Coppard, like
Lawrence, being a man of the people, knew what the
grindstone was, and when he describes people of his
own class, like Frank Oppidan and the Higgler, each
with his dream of a nice girl with a little money, the
personal freedom Coppard had himself achieved
gave him a new perception of the possibilities of their
lives; but when he turned it on people of the leisured
classes it tended to become a romanticism of wealth
and position. With Lawrence this doesn't really matter: the man was a flaming romantic anyhow, and I
find myself reading those later stories in which he
represents himself as a benevolent god, gamekeeper,
gypsy, stallion, or sunlight come on earth to relieve
wealthy women of their sexual frustrations as fairy-

tales, legends, prose poems—anything on God's earth
except a representation of human life and destiny.
But the thought of Coppard as god or gamekeeper
only makes me laugh. I see him squatting on a fence
after he had introduced me to a nice girl who had had
an unhappy love affair with a modern poet and hear
him say—referring back to an earlier argument of
ours—"And you think I'm unfair to modern poetry!"

In this metamorphosis Coppard's greatest virtues
become faults in their own right. His uncanny perception of a woman's secretiveness, her mystery, the
thing that lures men, continues, but the mystery
gradually seems to require a larger and larger income
to support it in the style to which it is accustomed,
until the dullest, plainest housewife begins to seem
more attractive. The quality—the packing of the story
with fascinating though largely irrelevant detail—becomes more irritating, as though Coppard were not
really performing an impudent pirouette but indulg-
ing some nervous tyranny. Freedom and necessity are
not abstractions but different poles of the human condition, and too much emphasis on one can only result
in some inhuman form of the other.

I should be surprised if life in the communist states
which attracted Coppard so much did not result in
some new sort of personal eccentricity, some sort of
erratic behavior that merely caricatured the behavior
of men and women in some country where—theo-
retically at least—they are free.

10. The Romanticism of Violence

THE TWO MOST remarkable storytellers of the
First World War were Ernest Hemingway and
Isaac Babel. It may be a slight inaccuracy to link
Babel with the European war when his connections
were mainly with the Russian Civil War, but the two
wars and the two men clearly belong together.

The two men have in common what I can only
describe as a romanticism of violence. Hemingway's
is clear enough. He never makes the mistake of cele-
brating "Mercy, Pity, Peace, and Love." The only
virtue he exalts is physical courage. In reading Irish
or Icelandic sagas we have to be prepared to exalt it
too, for, like patience and industry, it is a necessary
condition of existence, but our society has so con-
ditioned us that we tend to relegate it to policemen
and sailors, and even in wartime among the troops
there is no particular enthusiasm for the fighting
man who is superlatively brave. He is only too likely
to get his comrades into trouble.

This is what I call romanticism and Babel shares it

with Hemingway. One can only assume that the romanticism goes deeper than the mere accident of finding themselves either brave or timid in the conditions of modern warfare, and that it must be rooted in childish or adolescent experiences of suffering. One who in childhood has got himself the reputation of being a coward and in later life proves his own courage will naturally be inclined to attach more significance to it than the rest of us do.

What Hemingway's experience was we don't know, but it is easy enough to imagine that Babel's must be connected with the suffering and humiliation of a Jewish boy of genius in a half-barbarous society whose language gives us the word we use to describe anti-Jewish atrocities. Isaac Babel would have been a very queer Jewish boy—and indeed, a very queer boy—if he had not often imagined himself as the avenger with the gun.

And yet this fantasy contradicts something that goes very deep in the Jewish character—an instinctive apprehension that though money is excellent and power is good, books are in some way better; a conviction of the supremacy of mind over matter, of the word over the deed. That is why when a Jew turns vicious he turns very vicious indeed, because he acquires the dual character of a criminal and a renegade. Babel's romanticism of violence draws its intensity from the conflict in himself between the Jewish intellectual and the Soviet commissar. Only by romanticizing violence could he live with it.

Babel's most famous work is *Red Cavalry* (1926), a book of stories that influenced me very deeply when

it appeared in English. It is not his most characteristic
work, nor should I now say his best. There is more of
the essential Babel in *Odessa Tales* which appeared
in 1924, and still more in the occasional stories he
wrote before he was murdered by the Stalinists on the
outbreak of the Second World War.

The early stories already have something of the
highly formalized manner of the later ones and which
bears such a strong resemblance to Hemingway's
manner. Since neither could have been influenced
by the other we must trace the style of both to a common source, which is certainly Flaubert. Indeed, considering Flaubert's influence on the modern short
story, it would not be too much to say that he should
be considered among the storytellers. The extraordinary relationship he established between the object
and the style is almost unmanageable in anything so
long as a novel, but again and again in the short story
we see how it serves to delimit the form, establishes
the beginning and the end, and heightens the intensity that is so necessary in a story but so embarrassing
in a novel, where everything has to have a sort of
everyday quality.

In Babel's earlier stories we see much more clearly
the personal need that gave rise to them, and with it,
the slight element of falsity we have to correct, unless
we are prepared to make the mistake that Lionel
Trilling makes in his fine introduction to the stories.
Having quoted Hazlitt's remark that "we are naturally
drawn to the representation of what is strong and
proud and feral," Mr. Trilling replies that "we are,
rather, drawn to the representation of what is real."
Outside the sagas I am not very much attracted by

what is strong and proud and feral, but if I were dependent for my idea of reality on the Odessa gangsters of Babel I should be in a bad plight indeed.

Babel's gangsters are much less real than Hemingway's Chicago gangsters, for these at least have been observed at third hand through the medium of films or *True Detective* magazines ("Cardazzo, the pale-faced, soft-voiced Brooklyn kid, who killed slowly, lovingly, with carefully-spaced thrusts of the knife"), but Babel's gangsters never existed at all outside the wild imagination of a delicate, scholarly Jewish boy, who had been hunted through the streets like an old dog, and whose mind was full of pirates in gorgeous colors.

Take, for instance, the marriage of the gangster's sister, described in the Flaubertian Technicolor of *Salammbô.*

All that is noblest in our smuggled goods, everything for which the land is famed from end to end, did, on that starry, that deep-blue night, its entrancing and disruptive work. Wines from these parts warmed stomachs, made legs faint sweetly, bemused brains, evoked belches that rang out sonorous as trumpets summoning to battle. The Negro cook from the *Plutarch,* that had put in three days before from Port Said, bore unseen through the customs fat-bellied jars of Jamaica rum, oily Madeira, cigars from the plantations of Pierpont Morgan, and oranges from the environs of Jerusalem. . . . And now the friends of the King showed what blue blood meant, and the chivalry, not yet extinct, of the Moldavanka district. On the silver trays with ineffably nonchalant movements of the hand, they cast golden coins, rings and threaded coral.

Seriously, is this what Mr. Trilling calls "real"? "With ineffably nonchalant movements of the hand"?

But these gangsters are straight out of *The Beggar's Opera!* Look how Benny Krik, the gangster, writes to the unfortunate man from whom he is demanding protection money: "Highly respected Ruvim, son of Joseph! Be kind enough to place, on Saturday, under the rain barrel, etc. If you refuse, as last time you refused, know that a great disappointment awaits you in your private life. Respects from the Bentzion Krik you know of." Does anyone believe that a serious magazine like *True Detective* would even print such stuff as "real"? But there is much better than that. When one of Benny's gangsters shoots an innocent Jewish clerk during a holdup, Benny not only buries the victim in Hollywood gangster style but with equal pomp buries the murderer beside him. Then he delivers a funeral address over the two graves.

"There are people who know how to drink vodka, and there are people who don't know how to drink vodka but drink it all the same. And the first lot, you see, get satisfaction from joy and from sorrow, and the second lot suffer for all those who drink vodka without knowing how. And so, ladies and gentlemen and dames, after we have said a prayer for our poor Joseph I will ask you to accompany to his last resting place one unknown to you but already deceased, one Savely Butsis."

Now, anyone reading that passage might be excused for believing that the original author was Damon Runyon. But perhaps Damon Runyon was also a realist? I should describe it as Jewish humor at its dotty best and Ikie Babel as a liar of colossal genius, but please, ladies and gentlemen and dames, do not let us get our terms mixed up! Whatever it is, it is not realism.

This, of course, is not all there is to the *Odessa
Tales*. There are the stories of the pogrom of 1905,
and though I feel sure that Babel, being the romantic
he is, has dolled them up, they are too close to what
all of us know of the reality of racialism not to move
me.

What does concern me about these stories is something that is more important than the question of
whether we call them romantic or realistic. It is the
question of what the author's personality is really
like. There are two personalities in them, that of the
Jewish intellectual and that of the Soviet officer, and
while one seems to say one thing the other often says
the opposite. I am never quite certain which of them
I am dealing with—Ike Babel or Comrade Babel. "The
End of Saint Hypatius" is a typical post-revolutionary
Russian story as is "You Were Too Trusting, Captain"; so, almost to the point of caricature is "Line and
Colour," a contrast between the vague idealist, Keren-
sky, and that master of the precise phrase and the
revolver, Leon Trotsky. I am not quarreling with the
idea—if it is an idea—nor with its expression; I am
merely wondering what degree of importance I am
supposed to attach to it. Is this the expression of an
attitude to human life or merely a mood such as comes
over us all at times? I am confused.

I am not confused but confounded by "With Old
Man Makhno." In this a Jewish girl is raped by six
Russian soldiers in succession. She would have been
raped by a seventh except that the rape went by order
of seniority, and Kikin, the seventh, realized that in
the process she was being raped by another Com-

munist hero reputed to be a syphilitic and, so as not
to contract the disease, preferred to nurse a grievance
which he expounds to the poor child who has been
violated and infected by his comrades. At this point I
really want to be vulgar, whip out my notebook and
pencil, and ask, "Your point, Comrade Babel, your
point? Are you implying that this is a small, inevitable tragic accident such as is bound to occur with
Heroes of the Revolution, or do I detect a hint that
hanging—as in certain capitalist armies—might best
meet the case? Am I in fact speaking to Comrade Babel
or Ike Babel?" But Babel, like Hemingway, is being
so infernally tough that he leaves me in doubt
about a perfectly simple question as to whether I
should regard him as a real writer or as a dangerous
lunatic.

Of course, there is the possibility that this is a mere
failure in technique, but it occurs again and again.
The person I regard as the Jew and genius writes
"Karl Yankel" and "In the Basement," but in "The
S.S. Cow-Wheat" I am apparently expected to admire
the conduct of Comrade Makeyev who reluctantly
executes the drunken skipper of a boat that has been
commissioned to bring urgently needed wheat to the
Moscow region. This gives me the same sort of thrill
I experienced when Comrade Shaw described en-
thusiastically how Comrade Lenin enforced punc-
tuality on stationmasters by shooting them on the spot.
Unlike Comrades Shaw and Lenin, I have suffered
from stationmasters, and I think I know what can
happen in wartime as a result of inferior transport,
but I still feel that there are better ways of keeping
trains on schedule than by shooting the stationmasters.
In fact, unless Russian rail systems are far superior

to European ones, shooting stationmasters would be just as ineffective as flogging witches, which is what one of Turgenev's characters did when his enormous carriage refused to start. It is not only wicked; it is silly.

What does emerge from these brilliant stories is an impression of an extraordinary attractive mixed-up Jewish kid. I am happiest with the later stories which are much more overtly Jewish, like the one that describes how the inhabitants of the Old People's Home by the cemetery make a comfortable living by hiring out a coffin which is seized by the Communists. But once more it is not of Chekhov or Maupassant but of Damon Runyon that I think when I read the address of Broidin, the overseer of the Jewish Cemetery, to the old people who have lost their only means of livelihood.

"There are people who live worse than you, and there are thousands upon thousands of people who live worse than the people who live worse than you. You are sowing unpleasantness, Arye-Leib, and you will reap wind in the belly. You will be dead men, all of you, if I turn away from you. You will die if I go my way and you yours. You, Arye-Leib, will die; . . . and you, Meyer Endless. But before you die, tell me—I am interested in the answer—have we by any chance got Soviet power or haven't we? If we haven't, and I am mistaken, then take me along to Mr. Berzon on the corner of De Ribas and Yekaterininskaya, where I worked all the years of my life as a waistcoat-maker. . . ."

This is not "strong and proud and feral" or anything else of the kind; it is plain Jewish fun, and Babel is enjoying his own ability as a liar of genius. One must keep this in mind when approaching a book of stories like *Red Cavalry*. Mr. Trilling merely shrugs his shoulders at the protests of General Bu-

denny who, rightly or wrongly, regarded it as a libel
on his troops. I am not saying that atrocities don't
occur (I have seen one or two), nor am I arguing that
things were not infinitely worse in countries I have
not seen, like Poland and Palestine. What I am saying
is that when a Jew with an uproarious imagination
describes scenes of violence one should ask oneself
whether he is describing what he saw or what he
thought he should have seen. Some of the things Babel
describes I am quite certain he never saw. My own
experience of Jesuits and Jews has been moderately
pleasant, but as a reader of sensational fiction I realize
that my experience is nothing to depend upon, for in
sensational fiction all Jesuits are intriguers who have
love affairs with sinister society women and all Jews
people who drink the blood of Christian children.
Babel is a new experience to me, for in him I get a
description of Jesuits written by a Jew.

Bone buttons sprang beneath our fingers, icons split down
the middle and opened out, revealing subterranean passages
and mildewed caverns. The temple was an ancient one and
full of secrets. In its glossy walls lay hidden passages, niches,
doors that moved noiselessly aside.

O foolish priest, to hang the bodices of your parishioners
upon the nails in the Saviour's cross! In the Holy of Holies
we found a trunk with gold coins, a morocco-leather bag
with banknotes, Parisian jewellers' cases filled with emerald
rings.

I wish some Jesuit would write like this about the
synagogue. I know of one priest who puts up quite a
good show in his regular monthly tirade, but he is not
a Jesuit, and he hasn't the air of imbecilic rapture
which Babel adopts. But is it even necessary to be

satirical about this sort of thing? Can there be a
reader so guileless as not to wonder whether Babel's
Jesuit churches came out of Babel's experience or
his imagination?

But if the reader and I agree on where the churches
came from, what are we to say about the Russian
family background as it seemed to an Odessa Jew?
Dad, who has turned "traitor" and joined General
Deniken's army, captures a Communist detachment
which includes his two sons.

> And they took us all prisoners because of that treason and
> my brother Theodore came to Dad's notice. And Dad began
> cutting him about, saying "Brute, Red cur, son of a bitch!"
> and all sorts of other things, and went on cutting him about
> until it grew dark and Theodore passed away.

Now, we all know that in civil war father is often
set against son and brother against brother, and no
doubt from time to time they have killed one another.
(In fact, when I was a prisoner I knew a father with a
son among the guards, and when the father went for
a walk the son walked beside him outside the wire
and muttered, "Dad, Mother says how are you?" and
the father replied sourly, "Go away, you son of a
whore!") I have counted up in the pages of Maxim
Gorky the number of wives kicked to death by their
husbands, but I should still have said that this representation of paternal love was unique, even if it had
not been improved by the picture of filial devotion
that ensues, for Simon, Theodore's brother, in due
course captures Father.

> But Simon got Dad all right and he began to whip Dad
> and lined up all the fighting men in the yard according to

army custom. Then Simon dashed water over Dad's beard, and asked him:

"You all right, Dad, in my hands?"

"No," says Dad, "not all right."

Then Simon said: "And Theo, was he all right in your hands when you killed him?"

"No," says Dad. "Things went badly for Theo."

Then Simon asked: "And did you think, Dad, that things would go badly for you?"

"No," says Dad. "I didn't think things would go badly for me."

Then Simon turned to us all and said: "And what I think is that if I got caught by his boys, there wouldn't be no quarter for me. —And now, Dad, we're going to finish you off."

I do not think we should blame General Budenny too much, if, lacking an artistic training, he did not regard this as a tribute to his troops. I know a lot of officers, Irish, English, and American, who would have felt just the same.

This is not quoted to exaggerate the element of falsity in Babel's stories. He probably saw things more searing to the imagination than most of us have seen, and, anyway, he was working out an emotional problem that cannot be judged by the literal standards of General Budenny and Mr. Trilling. We can appreciate that problem in the story of how the narrator irritated his comrades by riding into battle with an empty revolver to make sure that no man's blood would be on his head. We can appreciate it even better in a story like "The Death of Dolgushov," in which the narrator during a retreat finds a mortally wounded man who begs to be dispatched before the enemy can torture him, shrinks away from the terrible responsibility, and as a result is himself al-

most murdered by his best friend, who having killed
the wounded man, says to the narrator, "You four-
eyed bastards have as much pity for your comrades
as a cat for a mouse."

There, certainly, speaks the Jewish idealist. Nor are
all the stories in which Babel celebrates physical
violence false and strained. There is nothing faked in
"The Death of Dolgushov" nor in another fine story
called "Prishchepcha's Vengeance," in which a young
Cossack whose parents have been killed by the Whites
goes from house to house, collecting the few family
possessions that have been stolen by unfeeling neighbors and killing the possessors; and then, at the end
of three days sets fire to his home and rides off. That
might easily be an incident in an Irish or Icelandic
saga and impresses us as the terrible incidents in these
do, without taking from our feeling of the common
humanity we share with their authors.

But I have no such feeling about the other story I
have quoted. However attracted a young Jewish intellectual may be by violence, a Jewish father who
had flogged his own son to death would not, shall I
say, receive an enthusiastic welcome from the community, and a son who had flogged his father to death
might even be treated with a certain reserve—at least
in the communities I know. I feel the story is literary
and faked in the same way as I feel that the description of the Odessa gangsters and the Jesuit church is
literary and faked. In his enthusiasm for Cossack
violence Babel has denied his ancestry.

For me Babel is always most moving when he remembers it and writes out of the conflict in himself,

when he juxtaposes the two cultures—the barbaric
culture of the Communists and the humane one of the
Jews—and shows them to us in antithesis.

His things were strewn about pell-mell, mandates of the
propagandist and notebooks of the Jewish poet, the portraits of Lenin and Maimonides lay side by side, the knotted
iron of Lenin's skull beside the dull silk of the portraits of
Maimonides. A lock of woman's hair lay in a book, the
Resolutions of the Party's Sixth Congress, and the margins
of Communist leaflets were crowded with crooked lines of
ancient Hebrew verse. They fell upon me in a mean and
depressing rain—pages of the Song of Songs and revolver
cartridges.

One can study the conflict best in a fine story like
"Squadron Commander Trunov," where the formal
construction is particularly revealing. Chronologically
the story tells how Trunov was killing his prisoners
and was rebuked by the Jewish narrator for not obey-
ing orders. A squadron of American planes comes
overhead, and Trunov and his buddy decide to try
and fight them off while the squadron escapes. Trunov
is killed and is given a hero's funeral with the fierce
Cossack rites, while the narrator, as though seeking
comfort for his own disturbed mind, drifts into the
Jewish quarter only to find the Jews there quarreling
about age-old points of doctrine.

A section of them—the Orthodox Jews—were extolling
the teachings of Adassia Rabbi of Belz. For this they were
being attacked by the Hasidim of moderate doctrine, the
disciples of Juda Rabbi of Gussyatin. The Jews were arguing about the Cabala, making mention in their discussions
of the name of Elijah, Gaon of Vilna and scourge of the
Hasidim.

Then in the place where a gypsy is shoeing horses one of a group of Cossacks attacks the Jew for having beaten up the hero Trunov that morning—a story we already know to be false, but the quarrel between the dead hero and the living Jew is becoming legendary.

It is a beautiful story that expresses allusively and movingly the tragedy of the idealistic Jewish lad who has abandoned his own people with their crazy religious squabbles in hope of a better future for humanity but will never be accepted by the wild Cossack throat-slitters whom he admires. It could have been told in direct narrative and chronological order as I have summarized it; it could have been told by a flashback from the wild funeral scene to the death of Trunov and then ended with the antithesis of the Jewish squabbling. Instead, because Babel decided to follow the line of his own troubled thought, it begins with the funeral, goes on to the argument among the Jewish sectarians, and ends with the quarrel over the murder of the prisoners and the heroic death of Trunov. Only in this audacious way could Babel have expressed without propagandist harangues his own final faith in Trunov and the heroic gesture.

There was, I suspect, a lot of Benny Krik in Babel, and he, too, for much of the time seems to have believed that "passion rules the universe." Accordingly, the stories in *Red Cavalry* contain more poetry than storytelling, which may be what I think is wrong with them. Passion can never rule the universe of the storyteller; it leaves too many things unexplained.

Nowadays, I prefer the later stories, like the enchanting Odessa story I have already quoted from, "The End of the Old Folks' Home." This, too, presents us with the antithesis between Communists and Jews, but a certain sly humor in it makes me wonder whether Babel himself had not begun to have doubts about the superiority of the Communists. They also left many things unexplained.

It is almost as though Babel had begun to realize that the uneasy alliance between the Jewish intellectual who went into battle with an unloaded revolver and Comrade Babel who had steeled himself to describe massacre and rape was coming to an end, and that Comrade Stalin whose purposeful prose he had so dutifully admired would soon deal with him and his kind with revolvers that were not unloaded.

11. *The Girl at the Gaol Gate*

T HE LITERATURE of the Irish Literary Renaissance is a peculiarly masculine affair, and I
fancy the same is true of most renaissance literatures.
Almost of necessity they are the work of men of action
disguised as men of thought, or of men of thought
disguised as men of action. In such reckless adven-
tures as donating a backward country with a literature it does not want, women must be left at home,
or, at most, be permitted to bring food to the prison
gates, because the explosion of a flying bishop can
do them so much more damage than it can do to men.
A man can live comfortably with little in the way of
society, but it is in society that women belong, and
it is in society that ecclesiastical shrapnel is most
effective. Lady Gregory, of course, was so much part
of the movement that it is impossible to think of it
without her, but it is also difficult to think of her as
a typical woman. I believe it is Yeats who tells the
story of how, when some patriotic soul threatened her
with assassination, she provided him with the perfect

occasion; someone else tells the story of how when O'Connell Street was cleared by Black and Tan machine guns, the old lady stood alone in the street, shook her fist, and shouted, "Up deh rebels!" and I remember myself how when a bishop blew up in her vicinity she merely sniffed and said, "Only anudder storm in a chalice."

So an Irishman, reading the stories of Mary Lavin, is actually more at a loss than a foreigner would be. His not-so-distant political revolution, seen through her eyes, practically disappears from view. She has written only one story about it—"The Patriot Son"— and from a patriotic point of view that is more than enough. It describes two young men, one a revolutionary, the other a mammy's boy who, despite his mother's scorn, admires the revolutionary from afar. When the revolutionary attempts to escape from his enemies, the mammy's boy tries to shield him, but all that happens is that he rips himself on some barbed wire and meekly returns to the authority of Ma and the local police. What the Revolution was all about was apparently the attempted overthrow of the Irish matriarch, a type Miss Lavin seems to dislike, and we may consider it a failure as the matriarch persists. The point of view is perhaps too exclusively feminine, for as the story unfolds, a man may be excused for thinking that the mammy's boy is a far better type than the revolutionary, Mongon, and might even feel inclined to pity any matriarch who in future tried to bully him.

But here, at least, the Irishman is on familiar ground, the ground of O'Flaherty and O'Casey. It is only when he turns to the other stories that he gets the real shock, for, though names, details, dialogue all seem of unimpeachable accuracy, he might as well be reading Turgenev or Leskov for the first time, overwhelmed by the material unfamiliarity of the whole background, versts, shubas, roubles, and patronymics. First, there is the sensual richness, above all in the sense of smell. "There was a queer pleasure, too, in smelling the children's soiled clothes and Tom's used shirts. Even the smell that would have turned her stomach as a girl had a curious warm fascination for her now, and in the evenings when the diapers were hanging by the fire to dry, with a hot steam going up from them, she shut her eyes and drew in a deep breath, and felt safe and secure and comforted." Even the word "diapers" in an Irish story is not more foreign than the feeling of that passage from "The Inspector's Wife." And surely, when one first reads Russian fiction, there is nothing in it more startling in the way of psychology than this from "The Nun's Mother."

Women had a curious streak of chastity in them, no matter how long they were married, or how ardently they loved. And so, for most women, when they heard that a young girl was entering a convent, there was a strange triumph in their hearts at once; and during the day, as they moved round the house, they felt a temporary hostility to their husbands, towards the things of his household, towards his tables and chairs; yes, indeed, down even to his dishes and dish-cloths.

As the last Emperor of Russia wrote in his diary on hearing of the Revolution, "Nice goings-on!" I remember my dear Lady Gregory, and the mighty end of "The Gaol Gate" and ask myself if this is indeed how most women feel. But then I remember also the girl from the North Presentation Convent who came to the real gaol gate with the cake she had freshly baked in the shopping bag on her arm, and, though she has been practically left out of modern Irish literature, I wonder if in fact this is not precisely how she does feel, and it seems as though a new dimension had been added to Irish literature. "O'Flaherty, L., *see also* Lavin, M."

Seeing also Lavin M. seems to raise in a more acute form the problems one had previously thought of only in masculine terms. To a great extent Yeats's early poems and plays had laid down the way that Irish literature must take, but in two books which once seemed to me to have had no real influence, George Moore paved the way for an entirely different sort of literature, and now I am not sure but that they have proved as influential as Yeats's. *The Untilled Field* is a collection of short stories, modeled on Turgenev's *Sportsman's Sketches* and intended by a Jesuit magazine to provide literary standards for young Irish writers. They began as simple little sketches of country life with no particular moral, but as he warmed to the job, Moore became more and more inflamed by the polemic that was his curse as a writer, and the stories gradually turned into a denunciation of Ireland and Irish Catholicism which was highly unsuitable for a Jesuit periodical. The other book was *The Lake,* a novel about a young puritanical priest who expels his amorous schoolmistress from her position, and only when she has emigrated realizes that he had acted out of jealousy and was really in love with her himself. In the beautiful close he leaves his clerical attire by the lake to suggest suicide, and swims away in pursuit of the schoolteacher and of his real nature. It is a magnificent theme handled in a finicking and tedious manner—ten years before, Moore, still in his naturalistic phase, might have made a masterpiece of it—but it is not the manner but the last few paragraphs that really raise in final form the problem of Irish fiction. What is settled in *The Untilled Field* has been established once for all by Joyce's *Dubliners* and O'Flaherty's *Spring Sowing*. Moore made the Irish short story a fact. But where are the successors of *The Lake* and how have they developed on and superseded their model? Most Irish novels still tend to end as *The Lake* itself ends, by the hero's getting out of the country as fast as he can. The only Irish novel that compares with it for excellence—Daniel Corkery's *The Threshold of Quiet*—ends with the heroine's going into a convent, which is only the same conclusion seen through a veil of resignation. There has been no development comparable with the development of the short story, such as would even make it possible for a critic to speak of the Irish novel, and the reason is plain. There is no place in Irish life for the priest or the teacher, no future for them but emigration, as in Moore, or resignation, as in Corkery. In the novel of his I admire most, Peadar O'Donnell describes a local shopkeeper's wife who secretly supports the young leader of the local co-operative movement in his fight against clerical and shopkeeping interests but who then remains on with her miserable husband. I argued with O'Donnell that she should have run away with the leader of the co-operative movement. O'Donnell replied—quite correctly I fancy—that she would not have done this. I argued—also correctly, I hope—that by this time it didn't matter what she would have done in real life. The logic of the novel had taken over. Neither of us, I think, mistook the other's point of view. We both realized that what I wanted was another version of *The Lake*. I was interested in his two characters as individuals, even if the community lost them. He, the more genuine novelist, was interested in the community and could not take the decision that would deprive it of the sort of men and women he admired. He preferred that life should go on underground.

Now, the short story *can* deal with life that goes on underground. You can write a number of stories about the life of Moore's hero which will ignore altogether the question whether Father Oliver Gogarty's duty to himself and society is not to find a nice girl and go and live in sin with her in Birmingham, and, because our Father Gogartys are often men of great nobility and distinction, you can even write of him with real beauty; but you cannot tell the full story of Father Gogarty's life, which, after all, is the novelist's task, without asking, "Was it worth it?" and the moment this question is asked it must be answered.

If I overstress this subject it is only because here, or somewhere about here, there should be a workable definition of the novel as an art form—a definition that would be useful to me as well as to others. If I ask myself whether a series of novels like C. P. Snow's *Strangers and Brothers* would be possible in Ireland I can only reply that I don't for an instant believe it. Why? Because the boys and girls could not gather around George Passant in a weekend cottage, or have love affairs, or discuss politics in public? It is partly that, of course, but only partly, for these are merely circumstances, and circumstances are much the same in most modern communities and merely express themselves in different ways. The real difficulty, as I see it, is that the narrator of these stories, who is partly Snow himself, though critical of English institutions and attitudes, is still very well pleased with things as they are, with what he regards as his own success, and so, ultimately represents what he and most of Snow's readers regard as a normal attitude to society. George Passant, Snow's finest character, a great man greatly drawn, fails not because of the Establishment or because of English provincial smugness or any other possible rationalization. He fails because of one small, barely visible weakness in himself, and Snow's narrator knows what the weakness is and can isolate it from all the possible accidents that might have accounted for it. An Irish Snow could never have isolated Passant's weakness, partly because the pressures on Passant would be so intense that it would be impossible to detach it from the weaknesses that would be caused by society, but even more because the narrator could never have regarded himself as representing normality. On the contrary, he would have realized as Yeats realized that he owed his position to having always been a bit of a freak and would have been drawn to Passant's weakness as much as to his strength.

But this is very much a man's argument. A woman cannot afford to caricature herself as a man may do, and if she does, she is made to pay for it. It is a drawback to the Irish woman writer. But, on the other

hand, a woman's ideas of success and failure need not
necessarily be the same as a man's. No man need regard himself as a failure if he has failed with women,
but a woman does so almost invariably if she has
failed with men. All through Mary Lavin's stories one
is aware of a certain difference in values which finally
resolves itself into an almost Victorian attitude to
love and marriage, an attitude one would be tempted
to call old-fashioned if it did not make the attitude of
so many famous modern women writers seem dated.
There is in the tone of the narrative even a certain
feeling of complacency, not at all unlike that of
Snow's narrator, but springing from an entirely different source. Take, for instance, that beautiful story,
"The Will." Lally Conroy, the bedraggled failure of a
well-to-do family, returns home for her mother's
funeral to find that her mother had died still hating
her and refusing to recognize her in her will. But
Lally is the only one who sees that it was her mother
who was the failure, who alone fears for her salvation,
and who insists on having Mass said at once for her
and on paying for it out of her own few shillings. It is
the bedraggled lodging house keeper who alone can
afford charity. We find the same reversal of values in
"The Long Ago," the story of three girl friends, one
of whom does not marry and continues to dream of
how nice it would be if only the husbands would get
out of the way and let them live together as they had
once been. When the husband of the second woman
dies and Hallie, the old maid, breathes this awkward
word of comfort to the widow, she projects an atrocious scene, a scene that for me at least weakens the
whole effect of a beautiful story. One can see the story

easily enough if one translates the values into male terms: the good-natured idler who, in comforting his successful friends for their reverses, presumes too far and slights the years of labor and achievement, but the reproof would have been quieter and more crushing. And again, it is the same sense of values that illuminates what I should now choose as probably Mary Lavin's finest story, "Frail Vessel." This is the story of two sisters, one of whom marries for convenience, the other for love. The prudent marriage turns out well, the love marriage turns out disastrously, and the frail vessel, Liddy, has to beg from her well-to-do sister, who is pregnant. By an exquisite touch of irony Bedelia, the hard woman, can still in feminine terms regard herself as the more successful of the two, but the moment Liddy reveals that she, too, is pregnant, Bedelia's whole façade of success collapses. Even penniless, homeless, abandoned by her ineffectual husband, Liddy carrying the child of someone she has loved is still the dominating figure, and nothing Bedelia can ever do will now alter that relationship between them. It is all very well for Miss Lavin to describe the triumph of a married woman on hearing that a young girl is entering a convent, but I get a strong feeling occasionally that her own rejoicing in the matter is not unlike that of the schoolgirl whose friend and rival in the struggle for the medal for French gets a prize for hockey instead. No more than the rest of us is she free of the Irish weakness for sentimentalizing religion, but there is an astringency in her treatment of celibacy which I do not find in any other Irish writer. Sometimes she counterpoints religion and sex, as in "Sunday Brings Sunday," in

which a pregnant little country girl has to listen week
after week to the maunderings of a half-witted priest,
and "A Wet Day," a brutal little story which I mis-
takenly chose to represent her in an anthology of Irish
short stories. Here, a parish priest, who is a monster
of selfishness, complacently congratulates himself on
having brought about the death of his niece's young
husband so as to preserve his own comfort.

That different set of values means that Miss Lavin
is much more of a novelist in her stories than
O'Flaherty, O'Faolain, or Joyce, and her technique
verges—sometimes dangerously—on the novelist's technique. That has its advantages of course. In her later
stories there is an authenticity and solidity that makes
the work of most Irish writers seem shadowy; not the
life of the mind interrupted by occasional yells from
the kitchen, but the life of the kitchen suddenly shat-
tered by mental images of extraordinary vividness
which the author tries frantically to capture before
the yells begin again. The only story in which she
deliberately eschews the physical world is the fable of
"The Becker Wives," which she sets in a capital city
that might be either Dublin or London, and among
merchants whose names might be Irish or English,
and, for all its brilliance and lucidity it seems to me
only the ghost of a story, a Henry James fable without
the excuse of James' sexual peculiarities. She has the
novelist's preoccupation with logic, the logic of Time
past and Time future, not so much the real short-
story teller's obsession with Time present—the height
from which past and present are presumed to be
equally visible. Sometimes she begins her stories too
far back, sometimes she carries them too far forward,

rarely by more than a page or two, but already in that space the light begins to fade into the calm gray even light of the novelist.

She fascinates me more than any other of the Irish writers of my generation because more than any of them her work reveals the fact that she has not said all she has to say. Between *Tales from Bective Bridge* published in 1943 and *The Patriot Son* published in 1956, her stories have developed almost beyond recognition, and with her growing power has come a certain irritable experimentation, as in "The Widow's Son," where she experiments dangerously with alternative endings and "A Story with a Pattern," where she experiments with the guying of her audience in the manner of Molière in "L'Impromptu de Versailles." Her most important work will, I fancy, be neither in the novel nor in the short story pure and simple. In the former she will be defeated by Irish society, whatever standard of values she chooses to judge it by, in the latter because in it she can never fully express her passionate novelist's logic. I should guess that her real achievements will all be done in the form of the *nouvelle,* in which she has done her finest work till now. But it will be a very different sort of *nouvelle,* as different from "Frail Vessel" as "Frail Vessel" is from the *nouvelles* in *Tales from Bective Bridge,* more expansive, more allusive, more calligraphic. In the remarkable group of stories of which "Frail Vessel" is one, there seems to be the material of a long novel of provincial life, put aside not because Miss Lavin lacked time or enthusiasm but because it would be bound to raise the question I have discussed about the value of lives lived in that particular way, yet which continued to haunt her because whether or not this was life lived as a sensitive person would consider it worth living, it was still life lived, and lived intensely.

Epilogue

THIS BOOK is mainly about past writers. I have tried to draw a few general conclusions from the history of the short story about what sort of art it is and where it may go. I have had to ignore my own experience of teaching it because this requires an approach that is different, personal, and perhaps without any general application at all.

When I began to teach story writing, I was not even certain that it could be taught. I soon realized that it could be taught, in exactly the same degree as painting, as a skill. Admittedly, I could teach it only in a manner that resembled my own, but once more I discovered that growing technical control soon makes an end of imitation, and scarcely does a young writer begin to feel confidence in himself than he works in a different way from his teacher. The stories of my students that I remember best only bore a faint general resemblance to my own and little resemblance to one another. By that time they were drawing upon their own experience, which was not mine.

It is easier, I think, to teach the short story than the novel; easier still to teach the drama. The short story and the drama have this in common—that there are certain subjects that are necessarily bad, so that one must give more attention to the subject and less to the treatment. The story, like the play, must have the element of immediacy, the theme must plummet to the bottom of the mind. A character is not enough to make a play; an atmosphere is not enough to make a play, for the audience falls asleep. It must have a coherent action. When the curtain falls everything must be changed. An iron bar must have been bent and been seen to be bent.

William Butler Yeats once said to a young dramatist, "Set your play first in tenth-century Byzantium, then in fourteenth-century Florence, then in modern Ireland, and if it remains equally true of all, write it." This seems like a rather pompous version of what he said to me, "If you want to write a play, write it on the back of a postcard, and I'll tell you whether we can produce it or not."

That, of course, is something no elderly novelist could say to a younger man, for ninety or more per cent of a novel is treatment. What could any practicing novelist have advised Thomas Hardy to do with a theme like *Far From the Madding Crowd* except to forget it? The novel is greater than the subject, or, rather, the novel has so many subjects that a novelist can afford to make a mess even of the principal one.

That is why I sometimes spent a month of teaching, restraining my students from writing and confining them to the elaboration of subjects written in four lines—five if they must be garrulous. Anything more is not subject but treatment. When they wrote, "Betty, a high school teacher, aged thirty-five and a talented artist, who for ten years has been married to a dull official of the Forestry Commission, falls in love with a young man who is the representative of an insurance firm," I knew I was headed for trouble the moment they put pen to paper. The story was already written in their heads, and there would be nothing for me to do but ask, "Is your high school necessary? Is your forest necessary? Is your insurance firm necessary?" The story was written, and written in terms of a particular person in a particular situation at a particular time, and ninety-nine times out of a hundred the author had forgotten what the theme was. I am not trying to suggest that the realistic description of character and background is unnecessary; as I have said about Hemingway's work any realistic art is a marriage between the importance of the material and the importance of the artistic treatment, but, for the young writer at least, it must not lose sight of the former. That is the significance of Yeats's advice— "Set it first in tenth-century Byzantium." Lacking a knowledge of Byzantium, few of us can do that, but we can, at least, isolate our subject and consider it as something that might happen outside twentieth-century Winesburg or Dublin.

It is true that Chekhov wrote stories that cannot be summarized in a few lines, but that is the very rock his imitators always perish on, for they forget that he also wrote hundreds of stories that can. The extraordinary formless form that he invented for the story and the play is the creation of a man who was a perfect master of the commercial short story and the music hall sketch. "I send you a pound of tea for the satisfaction of your physical needs" writes a character in one of the later stories, but the inarticulate loneliness of that line should not blind us to the fact that it is really a line from some slapstick comedy that is suddenly being given a new meaning.

I am sure of the wisdom of the advice I gave my students on this point—"Set your imagination free." I have never been sure that I was right in advising them not to begin writing even then, until they had first written two or three rough treatments, but this may merely have been to warn them against the sort of mistake I made so often myself.

The first question I have had to ask myself about a subject, having tried to assure myself first of all that I was not handling the theme of a novel by mistake, was, "Is this a *conte* or a *nouvelle?* Can it be handled in one quick scene, combining exposition and development, or do I isolate the exposition in the first few paragraphs and allow the development to take place in three scenes or five?" If, for instance, it is the story of a father's death, should I begin with the birth of his eldest son or with the actual death? I hate drama used for exposition because it invariably reminds me of the intolerable five or ten minutes at the opening of a well-made play in which the husband helpfully recalls to the wife that they have now been married twenty-five years and have seven children, the eldest of whom has just become an architect, the second of whom is attending the university to become a doctor, and so on. Drama is the proof that the writer offers of the truth of his narrative, and should be used only in this way. It should always have the electrifying effect it has in a Greek play when the voice of the Chorus stops and we see the specific illustration of what we have heard as poetic generalization. In storytelling the reader should be aware that the storyteller's voice has stopped. But if I decide that the development is best handled in three or four scenes, which scenes shall I choose and in which order shall I arrange them, for this will decide exactly where the light is to fall. As I have said in discussing Babel's "Squadron Commander Trunov," the three episodes are so arranged that the story expresses a meaning which is not necessarily part of the story at all. In fact, by a simple rearrangement of scenes it could be made to mean something quite different.

But the real reason for the advice I gave my students was that a young writer who is gifted at all has more genius than talent, and is liable to write passages or scenes of great beauty that really have nothing to do with what he wants to say. George Moore's enchanting description of trying to help the younger Yeats with his impossible play, *The Shadowy Waters*, is true of more than poets. There are always those beautiful passages that the young writer cannot possibly sacrifice, and in draft after draft of a story I have found that lovely unnecessary description of a Wisconsin twilight turning up to confuse me and the reader. As I have said, the good advice is more for my own benefit than the students, but I would still say that a writer should bank down his creative fire until he knows precisely the object against which it is to be directed.

After that, the rest is rereading and rewriting. The

writer should never forget that he is also a reader, though a prejudiced one, and if he cannot read his own work a dozen times he can scarcely expect a reader to look at it twice. Likewise, what bores him after the sixth reading is quite liable to bore a reader at the first, and what pleases him after the twelfth may please a reader at the second. Most of my stories have been rewritten a dozen times, a few of them fifty times.

Alas, it is a process that cannot continue forever, for words are finite things and even the loveliest poetry loses its magic in time, even for the man who wrote it, but in this imperfect world it is the nearest we can come to the pleasure of the immortals, who can forever look on perfect beauty without wearying of it.

FRANK O'CONNOR (pseudonym of Michael O'Donovan) was born in Cork, Ireland, in 1903. Though he says that he received no education worth mentioning he has spent a considerable portion of his life in educating others, and his present book is based on a course of lectures he gave at Stanford University in 1961.

Mr. O'Connor's first published book was *Guests of the Nation*, a volume of short stories. He later published novels, several additional volumes of tales, *The Mirror in the Roadway* (a study of the modern novel), verse, travel books, a study of Michael Collins and the Irish Revolution, and the autobiographical *An Only Child*. His latest critical book was *Shakespeare's Progress*. He has lived in the United States since 1952 and taught at Harvard as well as at Northwestern University. He is a Litt.D. of Dublin University. Readers of *The New Yorker*, *Holiday*, and *Esquire* are familiar with Mr. O'Connor's stories and sketches.

THIS BOOK WAS SET IN

BASKERVILLE AND BULMER TYPES BY

THE HARRY SWEETMAN TYPESETTING CORPORATION.

IT WAS PRINTED AND BOUND AT THE PRESS OF

THE WORLD PUBLISHING COMPANY.

DESIGN IS BY LARRY KAMP.